KITTY CORNERED

For more stories about Bob's cats,
please read *Enslaved by Ducks* and *Fowl Weather*.

Kitty Cornered

....

How Frannie and Five Other Incorrigible Cats
Seized Control of Our House and Made It Their Home

....

BOB TARTE

Algonquin Books of Chapel Hill   2012

Published by
Algonquin Books of Chapel Hill
Post Office Box 2225
Chapel Hill, North Carolina 27515-2225

a division of
Workman Publishing
225 Varick Street
New York, New York 10014

Published simultaneously in Canada by Thomas Allen & Son Limited.
Floorplan on page ix by Bob Tarte.
Design by Anne Winslow.

Library of Congress Cataloging-in-Publication Data
    Tarte, Bob.
      Kitty cornered : how Frannie and five other incorrigible cats
    seized control of our house and made it their home / Bob Tarte.
          p. cm.
      ISBN 978-1-56512-999-3
        1. Cats—Michigan—Lowell—Anecdotes   2. Cats—
    Behavior—Michigan—Lowell—Anecdotes.   3. Pets—
    Michigan—Lowell—Anecdotes   4. Human-animal
    relationships—Michigan—Lowell—Anecdotes.   I. Title.
      SF445.5.T385 2012
      636.80092'9—dc23   2011050250

10 9 8 7 6 5 4 3 2 1
First Edition

*To my sister Joan, who is generous enough
to have taken in twelve cats,
and to my sister Bett, who is sensible enough
not to have any.*

Contents

· ·

GROUND FLOOR OF A HOUSE OVERRUN BY CATS

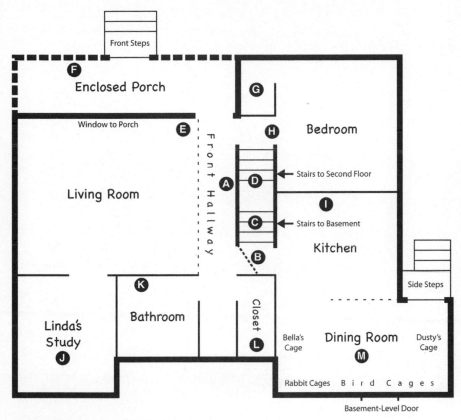

A. Inconveniently placed litter box

B. Confusing "closed-when-open" basement door

C. Daily attempts on Bob's life by Agnes

D. Decisive battle site in the War Between the Cats

E. Dining room chair commandeered by Lucy

F. Frannie's cardboard carton

G. Snoozing spot more comfy than Bob's shin

H. The funnel of happiness (location approximate only)

I. Carrots "too old for rabbits" cooked by Linda for Bob

J. Time-out for Mr. Cuddle-Wuddle

K. Shredded wallpaper

L. Sensibly placed litter box spurned by Lucy

M. Tina's under-table birdwatching spot

Cats of Characters

· ·

Agnes: our original cat who wonders where all of the others came from (*aka Aggly-wag*)

Frannie: nervous white-and-black stray who insists on being petted while she eats (*aka Alfalfa Girl, Ferret Face, Francine, The Little Kitty, Miss Pinkie-Winkie Nose, Sunday School Girl, Feline Trotsky*)

Lucy: snapping crocodile disguised as a "diluted tabby" with a disdain for litter box geometry (*aka Fatsy Pats, Lucy Caboosey*)

Maynard: portly tabby on a nonstop wailing expedition (*came to us as Mabel; aka Mr. Cuddle-Wuddle, Rand McNally, Harold the Barrel, Face*)

Moobie: aging snow-white cat who sleeps more than Snow White (*came to us as Moonbeam; aka "I Want," Conehead*)

Tina: thorn in Frannie's side with a periscope tail (*aka Teena-Weena, Periscope Girl, Tina Louise, Sis, Lump-a-Bump, Puppet Mouth*)

KITTY CORNERED

Introduction

· ·

I had my first encounter with a cat when I was two-and-a-half years old. It didn't turn out well. My mom had carried me next door so that she could get a closer look at our neighbor's climbing roses and still keep an eye on me. While she talked to Mrs. Farran, I busied myself by poking an anthill with a twig. Then I noticed the Farrans' black cat, Fluffy, rolling in the sun on the porch. Before anyone could stop me I lurched over and rubbed Fluffy's stomach. I enjoyed her promised fluffiness for a fraction of a second before a set of claws raked my arm. My howling ended the visit.

The incident didn't sour me on cats. It only made me wary of Fluffy. I was too young to develop prejudices yet, but that wasn't true of my parents, who held an unexplained grudge against cats. They had no problem with dogs—especially our family beagle, Muffin, who seldom stirred except to bury her head in her bowl. Cats, in contrast, were devious creatures, according to my mother. "You can't trust a cat," she said.

She repeated this for years. My dad backed her up. Finally, I asked him what was so bad about cats, and he told me, "They can jump on you and scratch you while you're sleeping." This was as close to spouting superstition as my commonsense father ever came, but I believed him at the time. I was in second grade by then and should have known better. But none of my friends had cats—or if they did, the cats were smart enough to keep out of sight when I showed up. So when I'd see a cat skittering across the street, I never thought of it as someone's companion. I thought of it as a wild creature like a squirrel or pigeon. A nuisance animal, in fact.

This all changed when I was in high school and my older sister Joan brought home a gray mass of matter fur from her riding lesson. "I named her Rigel, and I'll keep her in my room," she told my parents.

"Absolutely not," my mom said. "You're not keeping a cat in this house."

"What your mother says goes," said my dad.

Joan bought Rigel a litter box and set it up in a corner near her closet. She wasn't particularly rebellious, but her will to rescue a needy barn cat was stronger than my mother's will to keep out the cat. I sided with them against her, as I usually liked to do, but this time I really believed that she was wrong. Taking in Rigel was a betrayal of a family policy—especially from aging beagle Muffin's point of view. We were in for a surprise, however. Rigel turned out to be a shy and gentle soul who had zero disruptive impact on our lives. About the only time I knew that she was there was when I slipped into Joan's room to visit her.

Rigel was so sweet and undemanding that I ended up exchanging one false notion about cats for another. Instead of sharing my parents' belief that cats were trouble, I decided that they were hardly anything at all, just purring plush toys that wanted to be petted. Even Muffin seemed more intriguing. It never occurred to me that only a person who was duller than a sleeping dog would make such a mistake about a cat. I simply hadn't spent enough time around cats yet to absorb some of their smarts, or to know that each cat was different, and that some were considerably wilder and more unpredictable than others.

When Joan married Jack a few years later, Rigel joined Evenstar and Romulus in a three-cat household. When they took in a fourth cat named Tigger, I grew deeply concerned that Joan was suffering the dreadful fate of turning into a "cat lady." She and Jack had two dogs, too. But while owning a couple of dogs seemed normal to me, four cats struck me as borderline crazy. I figured that you might as well just move out into a hollow log as live in a house where there were twice as many cats as people. What was the point of four walls and a roof when nature had already taken over?

A decade and some years later, my thinking began to

change after I married animal lover Linda. Under my nose at first and then with my approval, our house filled with all manner of birds. For our first Christmas, she surprised me (to put it mildly) with a gray kitten that we named Penny. Before we knew it, stray cat Agnes needed a home. Moobie came next, and her arrival sent me to the store up the street for another litter box. When I complained about my fate to the cashier, she said, "Three of them. You must be a cat person."

"Not me!" I told her, as if she had accused me of running a meth lab.

By then I had long since recovered from my early misconceptions that cats were either devious creatures or as mellow as stuffed toys. There were both, and much more. In fact, they were as complicated as any person that I'd ever met and more intelligent than most people, too. But I refused to think of myself as a cat person. That was going a step too far.

I readily called myself a "bird person," because the term was so amorphous that it didn't pigeonhole me. A bird person could be anyone from an egg-headed aviculturist who specialized in rare parrots to a redneck with a backyard chicken flock. But the term "cat person" was pretty specific, suggesting a tame middle-aged eccentric who substituted interaction with pets for a healthy social relationship with other people. I resented that whole notion, because it described me perfectly.

I was able to console myself with the fact that the defining trait of a true cat person was living in an environment that was overrun with cats. We only had three, and the only reason that we had that many was due to a unique set of circumstances that had descended upon us like a dark cloud and could never occur again. At least that's what I told myself a few years before we ended up with six cats in our tiny house—including a wild child from the woods.

Perhaps I should have learned my lesson from Fluffy. And perhaps I should have listened to Mom and Dad. But I listened to my heart instead, and that always leads to trouble.

······························

CHAPTER 1

The Wisp of the Woods

Linda burst into the house in her usual door-knob-through-plaster fashion shortly after I had finished feeding Agnes. The floor bounced like a drum-head as she stomped the snow off her boots. Peering around the corner from the kitchen, I felt grateful that I wasn't still climbing the basement stairs, or the tremors might have pitched me off where an underfoot Agnes had failed. Linda tossed her boots onto the porch and then shucked off the pair of plastic bread bags that provided the waterproofing her thrift-store boots lacked.

"I saw that white-and-black cat again," she told me with the mixture of excitement and disbelief of a child glimpsing Santa Claus. "She was on the edge of the woods kitty-corner from the trailer park, but closer to us than when I saw her the first time I went to the store today, and I better not have forgotten to buy the shredded cheese again."

I went back to cleaning Bella's cage as Linda chugged into the kitchen. The parrot pinched my finger with her beak when I whisked her off the countertop to save her from getting clocked by a sack of groceries. "You have to be a better girl," I said.

"I couldn't see her very well through the trees," Linda said. "She was definitely after something and headed in our direction."

I pictured the stray running in that oddly unhurried but determined feline fashion: erect body, stiffly trailing tail, legs flickering like the frames of a silent movie. She trotted in a straight line toward our house until the honk of a diesel horn sent her scampering off in the opposite direction.

"She better not come here," I said.

Bella squawked to come out of her cage and resume her battle with an ice cube on the countertop. "Shh," I told her, leaning my face close to hers. "You're giving me a headache."

I loved our three cats, but I was a bird person at heart. Sixteen years ago, Linda had indoctrinated me into her world with an ever-increasing parade of fowl creatures who now lived with us, both inside and outdoors. And I'd discovered, after a long struggle, that I understood birds and their mysterious otherness. The cats had slipped in under the radar while we were otherwise engaged cleaning parakeet cages and making toys for parrots, and I'd assumed that in comparison to birds, they were the tame ones. The ones who basically followed domestic rules. Hadn't we always learned that cats were "domesticated animals"? I found more to laugh at than lament in naughty behavior from our birds. But I expected better manners from a fellow mammal and not the long stretches of brooding aloofness and general lack of gratitude of our cats. I wanted them either to act more like us or to play the role of cuddly toys, but time and time again they disappointed me on both counts.

"I forgot the cheese again," Linda said after pawing through two bags. In a noble, self-sacrificing, wounded tone of voice I volunteered to return to the store for her. But the errant cheese had become an orange badge of honor, and she resolved to retrieve it on her own. Moments later she thundered back into the house, an envelope of arctic cold clinging to her jacket as she kicked off her boots. Fortunately for her good mood—and for the church potluck supper—she had found the cheese inside the car skulking between the passenger's seat and the door.

In the kitchen, I watched her stash the cheddar in the crisper, where it was instantly swallowed up by a vegetative tide of "baby" carrots for Rudy the rabbit, hunks of ginger root for my tea, partially filled boxes of margarine sticks, shriveled flat bread, an empty plastic lemon, and, of course, another package of shredded cheddar cheese.

As I was taking inventory of the drawer, Agnes skittered up the basement stairs to rub against my leg until she had my attention. I turned toward her, and she trotted back down the stairs and stared up at me from the bottom. All I could see in the gloom peculiar to unlit basements was an incandescent pair of sulfur yellow eyes. Even in the full fluorescent light of indoor day, our black cat's facial features tended to merge into an inscrutable blur, especially compared to her inverse counterpart, the blindingly white Moonbeam, aka Moobie.

"I think she wants to go out," Linda told me.

"I think she's just angling for another treat." With Agnes safely planted at the foot of the stairs and out of range of tangling up my legs, I decided to make the descent, despite the futility of it all. To convince Agnes to come inside each evening, I had initiated the habit of rewarding her with a dollop of canned cat food. This turned out to be a huge mistake. She would beg to go out, come in, go out, and come in again several times a day in hopes of earning a spoonful of food, and darned if I wasn't weak enough to succumb to her sheer audacity.

This time, though, she didn't step outside by as much as a toenail. I opened the basement door, and a blast of Michigan air hit us like a frozen anvil. She pivoted, raced to her dish, and shot me her best "you might as well feed me" look. I scooped her up in my arms, rubbing her face in an attempt to rustle out a facial expression that I could see. I squeezed her and received the bleat of a crabby sheep in response. "I just fed you fifteen minutes ago," I said, putting her down next to her empty bowl.

But I failed to exercise necessary vigilance on my ascent.

Just a few steps away from the kitchen landing, Agnes intervened between my foot and the stair. I pitched backward trying to avoid her, my hand attempting to latch onto the nonexistent railing which I had been intending to have someone else install for years. Slamming my shoulder against the wall saved me, but I had come so close to falling that I felt the cold, clammy fingers of the cement floor reaching for the back of my skull.

Oblivious to my close brush with the reaper, Linda said, "I wouldn't be surprised if the white-and-black kitty shows up at our back fence."

I didn't give the matter a single neuron of attention. Once or twice a year, cats materialized in our yard only to disappear as soon as I opened the door and tried to engage them in conversation about how they needed to do something productive with their lives. These fleeting and possibly mythical creatures didn't much interest me, and a cat a mile away that I hadn't even glimpsed was completely off my radar, especially when we had a cat of homicidal bent literally underfoot.

"It's probably not a stray," I told Linda. "It probably lives with some long-suffering family at the trailer park who didn't realize what they were getting into when they took in a cat." I directed this last remark at Agnes, who had returned to the gloom of the basement to glare up at me from her bowl.

IN THE POST-POTLUCK DAYS that followed, as Linda rattled back to the store for soymilk, or to the post office for stamps with pretty flowers on them, or to the dime store for plastic wading pools for our pet ducks and geese, she saw the cat in ever-increasing proximity to our home. I feared that it was only a matter of time before the kitty would stumble onto the secret messages that other strays had left in the woods to guide more strays to our doorstep. In a language of scents and signs that only felines could decipher—an old mouse skeleton here, the heavily scratched bark of a sapling there—the cat calligraphy would tell her that in the blue house between the river and the road lived people who would shower her with food and affection—two softies whom even the dullest-witted critter could effortlessly wrap around its little toe.

Food and affection she would get, assuming she was just stopping by for takeout and not intending to reserve an inside table. We already had three cats, and we definitely didn't need a fourth. Agnes, Moobie, and our most recent acquisition, Lucy, gave us more trouble than our other fifty-some pets put together. I kept telling myself that their good qualities more than outweighed the negatives—just as I also imagined that our parrots were mild mannered and our geese as quiet as falling snow.

I hadn't grown up loving animals. In fact, I had been diffident to my boyhood beagle, Muffin. But marrying country gal Linda Sue seventeen years ago flipped on a switch that had been so deeply embedded in the whorls and dead ends of my fractured psyche that I'd never even dreamed it existed. Two of our first pets were profoundly unsuitable for companionship with humans. When we weren't besieging their previous owners for advice, we were trying to eject them from our lives, until we discovered that we had fallen hard for them. Belligerent bunny Binky and the Mussolini of "pocket parrots" Ollie relentlessly bossed us, but their sparkling personalities filled our house with jagged light.

My brother-in-law soon brought us a Muscovy duck that his co-workers had been pelting with stones. So more homeless quackers and consequent backyard pen expansions followed. Then came a quartet of geese abandoned in a roadside ditch, an increasingly affable succession of rabbits, African grey parrots, parakeets, doves, hens, and cats, not to mention the orphan songbirds that Linda raised and released each summer.

Though I might call any of them "baby," I never thought of our animals as surrogate children. I was the infant of the house, whiny, weak, helpless, crabby, and frequently in need of a nap. I was still trying to learn resilience from our pets, since the smallest bantam chicken was stronger, smarter, and more emotionally balanced than I was. But the best that I could muster was an extra smidgen of patience. I needed it to deal with the parrot who had devoured the dining room woodwork or the goose-size duck with the vice-grip beak who thrived on chasing us around the barn.

Mostly I loved our animals for their flighty yet constant companionship and the way their wildness was mitigated by an addiction to comfort. Dusty the parrot had learned to call Moobie by name. Rudy the rabbit had started mountain-goating up the backrest of the couch. Liza the goose stared longingly at the bowl of cat food that Linda had set for the white-and-black stray.

The kibbles went untouched. Then one afternoon the wisp of the woods became flesh and dwelled beneath our sunflower seed feeder, scattering the tree sparrows to the winds, and I grew alarmed. I didn't want her munching on wild birds that already had enough trouble surviving a cold and sunless winter.

She was white with mostly black hind legs that made her look as if she were wearing a pair of tights that were falling down. Her tail was black. A black continent floated in a sea of white on her right side, and a few black islands had broken off and drifted to her left side, shoulders, neck, and head. Although her eyes weren't large by cat standards, they formed an alliance with her pink nose to dominate her slender face when she peered up toward the house.

She looked smaller and more delicate than I had expected. The bright white expanses of her fur embarrassed the dinginess of the compacted snow, made the cloudy sky seem even gloomier. The flitting of goldfinches to and from the seed perches apparently didn't interest her, nor did a feeder-robbing squirrel who hung back behind the pump house flicking his tail as he scolded her. She seemed fixated on some other concern.

Her body twitched as she sat. It could have been a reaction

to the cold, but I feared that she was pretending to ignore the birds while on the verge of an explosive strike. I leaned forward to scare her away before she managed to snag a goldfinch. But before I could knock on the bathroom window she glanced up at me first with that heart-shaped face. One moment, she was crouching on the icy ground a leap away from the feeder. The next moment she was melting into the woods, running until her white-and-black coat faded to a gray smudge on the riverbank.

The merest flicker of eye contact had passed between us. But in the brief instant between the crouching and the rocketing away, as my cloudy blues met her metallic yellows, I felt the spark of a connection between us. It was a serious crush, though I had no idea at the time how deeply she would set her hooks in me.

Partly, she had moved me in the same way that any homeless animal would. But I also recognized a special quality in her that resonated with my own temperament. In my scant few seconds observing her, I had identified a kindred spirit, a creature who in spite of her many strengths was apparently as anxiety laden as I was. She was a shadow afraid of a shadow.

I told Linda about my encounter, leaving out the touchy-feely, neurotic aspects. "I put a dish of kibbles out for her in Don's driveway last night in case she didn't find the dish out back," she told me, referring to our former neighbor's empty house. "But it looks like a raccoon got to it first. The food was spilled all over the driveway and the dish was all chewed up."

I WAS ASHAMED of myself for blowing the white-and-black kitty's chance for an easy bowl of kibbles, but Agnes soon reminded me why I should be focusing on the trouble-makers inside the house. After ducking into the kitchen to retrieve my coffee from the microwave, I padded down the hallway toward Moobie. She broke off from noisily crunching on her food to fix me with a high-voltage "I Want" stare, intent on scoring a tastier morsel. Agnes was nowhere in sight—for the moment. Puffing on the hot handle of my South Dakota Badlands mug, I bent down to scratch the top of Moobie's head as I passed her on my way to check my e-mail. Then I took a fateful step around the corner.

Agnes, having overheard Moobie's noisy grazing, had po-sitioned herself on the other side of the wall and was lying in wait for her. My stocking foot unfortunately made an appear-ance first. Needle-sharp teeth pierced my skin. I went air-borne, ejecting a sparrow-size glob of hot coffee from my cup. The liquid hung in space, whistling a happy tune and biding its time until my as-yet-uninjured other foot moved directly below. Then it descended in a steaming splash. Deeply of-fended by my hopping and cussing, Agnes shot up the stairs.

After fortifying my feet with shoes, I felt contrite all over again about having uprooted the white-and-black cat. Al-though I couldn't make atonement to the stray, I could do the next best thing by apologizing to Agnes for spoiling one of her few indoor pleasures. Agnes was the embodiment of rolling-on-the-ground warmth if you encountered her outside in temperate months. But imprisoned inside the house during our endless winter, she got so grumpy that if someone substituted a wolverine in her place I wouldn't have noticed.

I discovered her curled up on my office chair doing her best impression of a life preserver. Her eyes shuttered open and regarded me warily.

"What a good, good girl you are," I said, and I reached out to stroke the curve of her back. Quick as a chameleon's tongue, a paw lashed out to bat my hand away. I had ignored the fact that Agnes could only be petted at certain times of the day, and only then if a particular set of legalistic conditions had been met. Although no one but Agnes had a clue as to what these conditions might be, a bad mood rendered every other consideration null and void. For failing to take her temperament into account, I had earned the exercise of her claws clause.

That night, just before Linda and I snapped off the light for an all-too-brief respite, Agnes leaped upon the bed and rubbed her face against my fingers. Complex feeding, watering, and out-of-cage shifts for our pets meant that there was barely an hour of daylight that didn't involve a task, although strangely I had discovered that I liked the structure that it lent my life. Each chore was like the picket of a fence that helped keep worry, obsessive thinking, guilt, and fantasies of success out of reach. But reliance on routine also made me less open to deviations from the norm, and I didn't embrace this unusual eleventh-hour interplay with Agnes.

She was insistent to the point of nuzzling my hand even after I had stuck it under my pillow, and one, two, three, or even fifty strokes weren't enough to satisfy her. She demanded to be petted, neck rubbed, and back scratched until she had covered my entire arm in an electrostatically charged coating of shedded hair. In the end I enjoyed it almost as much as she did. I could never look at a cat without longing to touch it, and Agnes had quenched my kitty-petting thirst far into the distant future.

"What a good, good girl you are," I told her as I hugged her, and this time she agreed.

As I squirted green dishwashing detergent on the living room rug and scrubbed our newest stain, Linda mentioned having seen the white-and-black stray eating from the bowl behind the fence. "I'm glad you're feeding her," I said, "But I don't want her hanging around all the time and thinking she belongs here. Next thing you know, she'll be throwing up on the carpet like Moobie."

"Did you give Moobie her hairball medicine?"

"I squeezed a slug into her food this morning. It's already gone."

Linda assured me that a stray cat this skittish would never come anywhere near us, much less amble indoors, confer with Moobie, and leave me a present to step on in the morning. Still, even the most misanthropic wild creatures sometimes developed a tolerance for humans when they needed help. We had experienced this with injured songbirds, hungry turkeys, and down-on-their-luck Realtors.

The past summer, a friend of ours had found a juvenile downy woodpecker on the ground after a storm and brought the tyke to us. He was already weak when we put him in our large outdoor flight cage. He refused to eat and spent every waking moment hammering away at the cage. Finally we opened the door and let him go, because there was nothing else we could do. Two days later, Linda's gardening helper said, "Did you see that bird on your wreath?" The little woodpecker was clinging to the plastic dollar-store flowers that adorned our front door. Back in his once-hated cage, he let me feed him with a syringe and by the next morning was eagerly pecking at a block of suet. After we let him go, he still frequented the yard, and he trusted us to come quite close while he was feeding.

So as I spotted the kitty hunched up against our pump house the following afternoon, I wondered whether the bitter cold might make her more people friendly. She was obviously lingering in our yard. I snuck a long look at her through the bathroom mini-blinds. Her face was beautiful, small and sleek like a ferret's and with a steely demeanor that had little in common with the complacency of a domesticated cat. She bristled with nervous energy. Even at rest, she seemed in implied motion and never relaxed her guard. But a divided cap of black fur on top of her white head undercut her serious expression. It reminded me of Alfalfa's slicked-down and parted hairdo from the *Our Gang* comedies and increased the inexplicable stab of affection that struck me as I stared. She seemed to sense that I was watching. I ducked just as she lifted her head toward the window, but not before I noticed a strange discolored strip that ran down her nose and lip.

I decided to venture out with food, so that she would associate me with something positive. I also wanted to get a closer peek at the mark on her face. After donning fifteen pounds of winter outerwear, gloves, boots, cleats, and scarves, I made my exit from the basement as unobtrusively as possible— softly easing the door open and letting her see my cherubic expression through the pickets of our gate. "Alfalfa gal, I've got food," I started to coo, but she wasn't ready for her close-up. Before I could get the phrase past my tongue she was already just a memory.

Over the next few days, I assured myself that I was simply indulging in the feline equivalent of scanning the snowy wastes for redpolls and other winter finches. But my thrumming heart gave the lie to my brain when I saw the stray at a distance stalking mice in our frozen swamp or skulking near a pile of branches where tree sparrows hid. The close encounter had evidently spooked her. Now she wouldn't come anywhere close to the house. Once, I caught her glancing up from our field to see my stick figure in the dining room picture window, and even that lo-res view caused her to high-tail it. Churning up a spray of ice crystals in her wake, she tore across the tundra racing all the way to the river, where a trickle of unfrozen water might wash away the hideousness of the sight.

LATER THAT WEEK, the day started with a bang. A crash like a meteor hitting the house jolted us as we ate breakfast. Ice blocks weighing ten, twenty, fifty pounds, or one hundred tons thundered, rumbled, and scudded down the roof, exploding on the ground with crater-forming intensity. An alienated chunk would occasionally teeter on the edge of the second-story roof and drop straight down to wallop the first-story roof directly above my head as I cringed with a bowl of grits. The terrified parrots flapped their wings, hovering inside their cages as if they occupied a falling elevator.

The massive berg-size rectangles of ice on the ground reminded me of the ruins of an Aztec city. "I'm glad the geese weren't out in the yard," Linda said, shuddering. "Or The Little Kitty," which was how we had started to refer to the stray.

"I'd better stay home today," I told her as I pushed a lump of grits from one side of my bowl to the other. "I'll be killed walking out to my car."

"I don't think a thaw is a reason to skip work."

As I ducked out the door, rivulets of water funneled down a row of icicles under the eaves and onto my head. Our skating-rink driveway had turned into a bog of slush. It would be thunderstorming by evening, according to our weather radio. While this wasn't what you'd call bikini weather—at least not for me—I welcomed any respite from winter misery. But later that day as I wrote sales copy for my employer's hi-fi products website, waxing poetic about a pair of loudspeakers that cost more than my car, I fretted about the stray. I wondered what she would do if she got caught in the rain and the flash freeze that was predicted to follow.

I worried about Linda's safety, too. We'd be pratfalling as we struggled with our outdoor chores the next day. I wasn't concerned about myself. I moved too slowly to easily slip on the ice; when was the last time you saw a slug lose its balance? But Linda always scraped her feet, and she had worn her boot cleats down into polished bumps.

Home for the day shortly after lunch, I had a plan to wrap a few strips of fencing around her boots as a makeshift traction device. But Linda was just back from her chiropractor, and I could tell that she was bursting to share a piece of news.

Linda's chiropractor was located midway between Michigan and Ulan Bator, and he was the only chiropractor in the northern hemisphere who could fix her up. Since she couldn't drive herself much farther than down the street due to her sacrum slippage, every Monday her friend Jan drove the sixty-mile round trip as Linda lay flat in the aptly named backseat.

"Jan dropped me off, and I was standing outside talking to her, enjoying the sunshine, when I felt something rubbing up against my leg. I looked down, and guess who it was."

"Agnes was in the front yard? She knows better than that." We didn't mind our cats losing themselves in the mud, weeds, and impenetrable thickets that lay between our house and the river. But we didn't want the cats anywhere near the busy two-lane road out front.

"No, not her. Agnes is waiting for you in the basement. It was The Little Kitty. Miss Run-If-I-See-A-Face."

"The white-and-black cat? Are you sure it was her?" I couldn't imagine our fraidy-cat rubbing against someone's leg. And if she did, why didn't she choose the leg attached to the person who was every bit as anxiety laden as she was and who carried her around in his mental worry bucket like a precious gem?

"She was rubbing against my leg and even let me pet her. She might be still around."

I tried not to judge my wife too harshly. I'd been reading how polar explorers subjected to prolonged periods of sensory deprivation often suffered from delirium, and our winter had been brutally cold, unusually snowy, and extensively icky even by Michigan standards. Plus, she had been living with me for over fifteen years, which would send anyone over the edge. She had probably encountered a frostbitten squirrel or, more plausibly, the Bigfoot-like creature that I believed inhabited our woods.

JUST BEFORE DINNER, as I trudged toward the barn carrying a bucket of table scraps, the scaredy-cat darted out from under one of our monster pines and then began a full-body massage to my booted calf. She cupped my leg beneath her chin, bumped me with her hip, and snaked her tail around my ankle before making a U-turn and doing it all over again. I wondered how this could be the same high-strung beast whom until this very moment I had only been able to glimpse like a holograph. She certainly seemed real enough. She purred and rubbed her head against my hand just as Agnes would, arching her back and halving her length as I stroked her.

"I wish we had room for you inside," I told her. I took a mental inventory of spaces in the house currently unoccupied by cats, birds, or rabbits. A few dresser drawers and the wastebasket in my upstairs office were all that I could come up with. "Maybe we can set up a bed for you in the barn. You'd like that better anyway."

I had imagined that her fur might be coarse and matted from the hardships of living outdoors, but she felt as luxuriously soft as any house cat. Then the house cat underwent a sudden transformation. Shifting her weight to her hind legs, she raised her nose and every nerve ending in her body went on alert, from the slits of her eyes to her cocked tail. For a moment she inhabited a world that I knew absolutely nothing of, a realm far older and deeper than my plodding-out-to-the-mailbox-for-the-daily-bills existence. Then, just as effortlessly, she came back to Planet Bob. The feral look slid from her face, the tension exited her body, she went back to rubbing against my leg, and I went back to petting her.

I sunk into an approximation of bliss, but not for long. A cat as distrustful of humans as she had been would only resort to intimate contact out of desperate need. I squished through melting snow back to the basement, dipped a plastic margarine dish into a bag of cat food, and pushed it under her snout. Then I stood by with grandfatherly pride while she vacuumed up the food. She danced tight circles in appreciation before zipping back beneath the evergreen—leaving me with an ungloved outstretched hand and nothing to pet except our propane tank.

Tossing spaghetti, potatoes, and chunks of bread to our mysteriously fat ducks and hens a few minutes later, I thought about the discolored strip of skin across her muzzle. I wished that she had followed me into the barn so that I could shelter her from the coming weather and whisk her to the vet if necessary.

Shortly after dinner, as Agnes waited for my feet to hit the basement steps, I carried an empty plastic pitcher through the living room and out onto our front porch to refill it from our refrigerator-size sack of kibbles. The television blaring from the other end of the house warned me about the 80 percent chance of precipitation after midnight. Rain had already started to fizz against the sidewalk. How would the white-and-black cat fare in the downpour, I thought, and then jumped back as I noticed her peering in at me, her paws propped against the aluminum door.

"Sorry, honey, you can't come in," I told her, though I had already opened the door. She shot onto the porch, but it was obvious that she was going through an internal tug of war. Before I could close the door again, she bulleted back outside then turned to stare up into my eyes with a sweet Sunday school expression. "You can stay out if you want to," I told her. She emitted a squeak so high pitched that if I hadn't seen her open mouth, I wouldn't have believed that she had made it. I held the door for her again, shutting it immediately when she popped inside—only to be chastised with the same plaintive *eek*.

A more patient man might have played doorsy with her for the rest of the evening, but there was a ceiling in our bedroom that needed staring at. I grabbed a gallon jug of alleged spring water, propped open the door with it, and retreated into the house. The cat hopped out into the downpour but darted in again by the time I had returned to the porch with a dollop of budget-price canned cat food. I touched her as she gobbled up the fish by-product and filler. As she raised her back to meet my hand, her whole body trembled. This wasn't the take-charge cat that I met in the yard a couple of hours earlier. This was a nervous kitty that felt confined by our porch even though she had a ready exit.

I wasn't surprised when she slipped back out into the rain after she finished eating. But I was floored by what happened next. She popped in again when I presented her with another helping of food. And instead of wolfing it down at once, she raised her head and fixed me with a look whose meaning I somehow understood. Despite her deep uneasiness, she wanted me to pet her while she ate.

It was almost more than I could stand. Her intensity. Her

conflict. Her fear. Her hope. Our cat-food bills. Tears came to my eyes.

I WAS NEARLY as conflicted as she was about her presence on the porch. It wasn't just a matter of adding another cat to our house. It was my concern about the kind of cat she was. Over the years most of our cats, birds, and bunnies had been sweet. Others definitely occupied the bitey, noisy, cantankerous, or just plain irritating side of the teeter-totter. But we had never knowingly taken in a difficult animal. We may have been softhearted, but we weren't full-blown crazy. And while it may have been written in the stars that some pets would bring us trouble, it hadn't been written in their faces when we first met them, or we never would have brought them home.

The white-and-black cat was different. She was already in our home, and she had already proven that she was difficult by being demonstrably more intelligent than I was. Had I been faced with the magnitude of problems that confronted her—homelessness, hunger, a possible infection or injury, and the imminence of freezing rain—I wouldn't have had the presence of mind to seek out the most logical people who might help. I would have fallen to the ground, tucked my head between my knees, and given up. That's just the kind of man I was. Without the talking-moose weather radio or the people on television, I never knew when rain was coming. I barely knew day from night. The prospect of having a cat around who would beat me in every battle of wits, including weather prediction, was daunting. But there she was on our porch.

Then there was her emotional intensity. Compared to my single kazoo note of anxiety, she was an entire orchestra of skittishness, suspicion, wariness, and premonition zipped inside a cat suit. It wouldn't be easy to deal with such a temperamental being. And speaking of temperamental, our sweet white cat Moobie had recently undergone surgery to remove a tumor from her shoulder. Fearing that we might lose her was bad enough. But during her recovery she had become even more of a demanding diva than usual, bringing persnicketiness to new extremes—even for a cat. I still hadn't recovered from the psychologically draining experience of catering to her whims, and by every indication The Little Kitty would be even higher maintenance. But there she was on our porch. And off our porch. And on our porch again.

Although these factors argued against keeping her—assuming that she was capable of being kept—there was another big fat reason for being hesitant about taking in another cat. That was big fat Lucy, our third, most recent, and most vexing feline addition to the house. But I didn't even want to think about Lucy and spoil the moment as I peeked out onto the porch and saw The Little Kitty peering back at me. I melted. I wanted what was best for her as long as this meant staying with us and using the porch as her headquarters for chipmunk search-and-destroy missions. I didn't want her to vanish into the trees.

She tilted her head, and her face fleetingly resembled a dozen different animals: a flying fox bat, weasel, bush baby, panther, lemur, spotted gecko, *Our Gang* star Carl "Alfalfa" Switzer, and obscure creatures I didn't recognize. Way in the back of my mind I saw myself easily transforming her into a fat and lazy pet who would snooze away the afternoon with me. I didn't know, of course, what a wild ride the wisp of the woods would take us on. By opening the door to her I had opened our lives to a whole new level of catdom.

....

CHAPTER 2

Dark Hour of the Walleye

I t was still raining cats, dogs, and something that resembled water when I peered out at the stray a few minutes before bedtime and found her stretched out on the porch floor.

"She shouldn't sleep on the cold cement," Linda said. She had never said that about me.

Grabbing one of the many pillows that she had consigned to our closet because it had failed her in the softness, hardness, thickness, thinness, or noncrinkling department, Linda set it on top of a cardboard carton. The white-and-black kitty took to the spot at once, curling up on the pillow for several seconds before ducking out the door to make sure that her passage to the outside world remained. Then she trotted back inside with a sheen of droplets on her fur.

As Linda yanked down the bedcovers a room away, I

fumbled at the door to stare out at the kitty. Next to the door on a wooden chair sat Lucy. I could see Lucy, but I could hardly see the chair. The massive cat watched me work the little locking thingy on the doorknob through slitted eyes that boasted wisdom, satiety, and the urge to bite. She lifted her head an inch off the seat cushion, and though I knew exactly what to expect, I took the bait and scratched her neck. She scrunched up her face with pleasure, all the while angling her hippopotamus mouth up until I could see her jaw as it tensed on the verge of a strike. I slid my hand down her shoulder. She pivoted her head and licked me once, then twice, before flicking my hand with a fang as I jerked away. Her beatific face positively glowed.

A vet once described Lucy's coloration as "diluted tabby." Imagine the world's cheapest dish towel, like the kind that I'd give Linda for Christmas. The stiff white surface is boldly printed with the image of a tabby cat, complete with an *M* on the forehead and bull's-eye whorls on the sides. Somehow the towel gets caught under the washing machine agitator and finally wiggles free after two thousand wash cycles. The faded blur that remains—ghostly gray with hints of brown and a few dull splatters from bleach—resembles Lucy's twilight tones, complete with a vague *M* on the forehead. To make the resemblance nearly perfect, stretch the fabric in whatever direction significantly expands the girth. Then sew on a set of false teeth that catch on your skin whenever you touch the towel.

Empress Lucy surveyed her kingdom from the dining

room chair. I had dragged it into our seating-challenged living room the previous Christmas when my sisters and their husbands were visiting. The chair was only supposed to rest near the door for a few hours before scooting back to the end of the dining room table. But as my sister Bett ducked into the kitchen for a plate of molasses cookies to pass around, Lucy pried her bulk up off the floor, shifted it to the chair, and growled when I attempted to shoo her away. I hadn't dared to move it back ever since.

As I ventured another scratch beneath her collar, I thought of how I couldn't conceive of two more dissimilar cats than the skittish waif on our porch and the sea lion on our chair. Even though the stray and Lucy were as different as night and not-night, they had one thing in common that gave me pause. Both of them were cats, and every cat that we had ever taken in was crazy. Sometimes we got lucky, and the good qualities far outweighed the bad, as with the sweet but demanding Moobie. Other times things went sour, and we got stuck with a big fat nuisance like Lucy, whose only positive contribution was to serve as a bad example. The old saying "once bitten, twice shy" was literally true with her. Although Lucy and I had worked out our major differences, she was still a strong argument against ever taking in another living creature. I didn't even want to gamble on a fern.

THE DAY THAT I decided to adopt Lucy is seared into my brain like my first morning at kindergarten, the disastrous

junior high date with Monica Plumb, and the Tom DeLay episodes of *Dancing with the Stars.*

That morning I awoke in a rare good mood to the distant sound track of Linda emptying the dishwasher. I would
spring out of bed to help her, I decided, even as I burrowed
deeper into the covers and considered the dining pleasures
that awaited me that evening. It was the day of the office
Christmas party, an event which I had scrupulously avoided
for nine years. But the previous year I had attended on a
whim, partly to satisfy my curiosity about my fellow workers'
spouses, but mainly because the Italian restaurant where the
party was being held was only fifteen minutes away—thus
satisfying my primal urges for food, companionship, and not
driving far. I hadn't intended to enjoy the party, but it happened anyway. My boss and his wife had turned out to be excellent hosts, and the pan-fried walleye was equally engaging.

As I luxuriated under a pile of covers, a cat vaulted up the
foot of the bed, strolled along the length of my body, and
planted its paws firmly on my chest. I opened my lids to the
blazing light of Moobie's eyes bearing down on me. Fearing
a radiation burn, I extracted an arm from beneath the quilt
and petted her. Purring noisily, she moved out of reach and
sat down, straightened her upper body, and poured every erg
of her life force into a stare that jarred me even through the
sheet stretched over my face. I could easily resist Linda's early
morning stirrings. But Moobie's summons was impossible to
ignore. I jackknifed out of bed and promptly filled her feed

dish before playing a round of dodge 'em with Agnes on the basement stairs.

I didn't eat much for breakfast, because I wanted to stay hungry for the party—plus, we were having grits again, which I enjoyed only slightly less than a heaping bowl of sand. At work I decided to skimp on lunch and squirreled away my windmill cookies for another day. Web designer Dave sat across from me. I had never met a more affable soul and figured he'd be thrilled to discuss the pan-fried walleye with me. Strangely enough, he didn't have his mind on dinner at 8:18 AM and wanted to prattle on about losing his house instead.

"We're moving," he told me. "Neighbor Girl's bought a gun."

Dave frequently regaled me with tales of his crime-ridden neighborhood. There was Neighbor Girl, the fifteen-year-old who sneaked out of her parents' house in the middle of the night only to wake everybody on the block with her boyfriend's muscle car. There was Redneck Guy, who hogged the driveway he shared with Dave. And he often told me about his cat, Lucy.

"I was wheeling my computer chair back to my desk, and Lucy jumped up on it. She'll also jump into a laundry basket if I'm dragging it across the floor. She'll ride on a rug, too."

Our cats hated anything involving motion not of their own making. Dave also told me how Lucy would beg and beg to go outside, only to park herself on the porch barely six inches from the front door. "She'll sit there for hours watching cars go by. If she sees a rabbit or a squirrel living it up, she'll watch more intently, but she's too fat and lazy to run after it."

Lucy seemed like a healthy alternative to Agnes, the bane of our local chipmunk population. I'd hoped to meet Lucy someday. I'd filed away the idea along with other vague plans like digging a heated tunnel to our barn or staying in a good mood for an entire hour.

"Why did Neighbor Girl get a gun?"

"Their house was broken into."

"So your house could be next."

"I'm more afraid of Neighbor Girl. I'll be emptying a wastebasket some night and have to throw myself behind the garbage can when she opens up on me."

Now he and his wife were going to have to ditch their rented house in favor of an apartment in a safer part of town. But the landlord didn't allow cats. And then, he said, "My dad changed his mind about taking Lucy, so she'll have to go to the animal shelter."

I had hated the thought of a pampered, eight-year-old computer-chair-riding cat ending up in a shelter. Surely we could make room for her at our place. I had a motive other than simply doing a good turn for a fellow animal. At fourteen, Moobie wouldn't be around a whole lot longer, and she was the nicest cat I had ever met. While friends, relatives, and everyone I bumped into at the local feed mill bragged of having a cat that sailed into its twenties, we hadn't been so lucky. Our first cat, Penny, had suffered a seizure when she was Moobie's age and had used up all her lives in a matter of a few seconds. Although Moobie was irreplaceable, I wanted a touchy-feely cat on hand to help soothe our eventual loss of her.

"Is she affectionate?"

"Very," he had assured me.

Later, after living with Lucy for a while, I realized that I should have pressed Dave as to how he defined the term.

BUT THAT DAY, two thoughts fought to dominate my limited attention span as I trudged out to the barn. The more important of the two was broaching the subject of Lucy with Linda. Much more trivial, and therefore significantly more magnetic, was the rapid approach of the hour in which I would leave for the office party. I didn't get out much, especially for dinner. Due to Linda's chronic back problems, we seldom engaged in public activities that required sitting. Restaurants were out, and so were concerts, movies, lectures in unknown languages, and go-kart racing, unless I attended these alone. And what fun is solitary go-karting?

Images of Uncle Sonny's Italian Villa beckoned like a fragrant flower. "What exactly do you suppose a walleye is?" I asked Victor, our head Muscovy duck, as I herded the ducks and hens into the barn. "It isn't a very flattering name for a fish. What if I called you 'caruncle-beak'?"

Victor threw his head back, opened his jaws like an alligator, and panted, giving my questions the contempt they deserved. His fleshy face mask—which a duck expert had graced with the pithy-sounding term *caruncle*—seemed redder than usual. Ramone, an uncharacteristically shy member of the same fraternal order, hung back in the barn from the undulating mass of ducks and hens awaiting their late-afternoon treat. Apparently he'd been picked on. I suspected that Victor was the culprit, although Ramone was always a bit more skittish. That level of baseless anxiety made the two of us soul brothers, so I tried my best to make sure that he received his share of table scraps. Tossing fruit his way was fruitless, however. The cut-up grapes, mixed with cooked corn and peas, sent a tide of gabbling fowl sweeping toward him, and he retreated into the gloom.

"You're not going to miss this good food, not tonight of all nights." In hopes of distracting the feathered piranhas, I tossed a handful of grapes and veggies to my immediate right, then arced a second handful far back toward Ramone, but this only succeeded in creating two phalanxes of ducks and hens. "You'll go to bed hungry," I warned, but he failed to rally. I completely understood.

BACK IN THE HOUSE, I peeled off my boots, stocking cap, gloves, and jacket, decreasing my body weight by 72 percent. I kept an eye out for Agnes as I climbed the basement stairs, moving slowly enough to allow myself a moment's preparation before I broached the Lucy topic with Linda. Early in our marriage, before we had started giving orphan ducks, geese, and hens a home, Linda had been the one to introduce animals into our house. Sometimes she succeeded by persuasion, as when she had talked me into getting grumpy bunny Binky. At other times she got critters in the door via artful smuggling, as when she presented me with Howard the dove on a wedding anniversary or Chester the canary on my birthday.

Over time, I had developed a soft spot for them that was coincidentally the same size as my head. I loved their attentiveness, the grace with which they dealt with problems, their tenacity, and just about every other attribute they had that I lacked. Furthermore, animals were just plain affectionate, including parrot Bella who was always demanding neck rubs. I had been the instigator of Bella's addition to our family, and now I needed to lobby for Lucy. Linda did both the lion's and the lioness's share of the work caring for our animals, and adding one more critter might push her over the edge.

As I squeaked open the door from the basement, I could tell that Dusty had put her in a mood that wasn't what you'd call pet friendly.

"What's going on?" I asked. Dusty's cage was shrouded with his overnight cover. He peered at me through one of the holes that he had chewed in the dark green sheet.

"He won't let me cook dinner. Because I'm in here, he thinks I have to do something for him every minute." That explained the parrot shrieks I had heard outdoors on my way back from the barn. Howard the dove landed on her head as she complained about Dusty. "These animals!"

"Speaking of which . . . There's a guy at work who has to put his eight-year-old cat Lucy in a shelter," I said, beginning to ever so slowly lay the groundwork for the case I intended to build. "He's moving, and his new landlord won't let him have any pets."

"Maybe we should take her," Linda said, deflating my argument in one fell swoop. "What's she like?"

"Well, Dave says she's very affectionate."

"Find out if he'll let us have her."

"I'm sure he will. But you don't think adding an extra cat will cause trouble?"

Behind the bed sheet, Dusty managed to free his bowl from its clamp and throw it explosively to the floor, spraying seed shrapnel in every direction. Linda shut her eyes and didn't say a word for a moment. Howard the dove clung to her hair.

"Anything but another bird."

Anxiousness nibbled at me as I headed for the restaurant. Few things happened in my life without an overlay of unease. Humdrum events like waking up in the morning, shopping for kitty litter, or opening an e-mail all troubled me to varying degrees. Arriving at a party was fraught with potential mishap. What if I strolled in too early and bore the disapproval of a waitress? Just as bad, I might be a tad late and doomed to wander from table to table searching for my candy cane–emblazoned place card.

The weather contributed to my sense of impending faux

pas. It was snowing, and since I didn't see well after dark under dry conditions, the wet precipitation turned me into a menace. The reflections of headlights, stoplights, and convenience store signage in the slick pavement addled my brain.

My thoughts turned to Lucy and her fate if we didn't take her. The shelter was a one-way trip for the majority of animals. Only the cutest, friskiest cats and dogs ever made it out of there—not a placid eight-year-old fatty, no matter how affectionate Dave said she might be. I couldn't let that happen, and I wondered what it meant that I couldn't let it happen to a cat I had never laid eyes upon. But it seemed like a small enough deed to do for a fellow creature, especially one that might hop up on my lap while I read a Perry Mason mystery.

I collided with the frozen smile of the hostess at Uncle Sonny's Italian Villa. I realized that I had made a mistake. My co-workers were in full celebratory mode somewhere else. Acting out of habit, I had decided that because the party had been held at Uncle Sonny's last year, it would be ever thus. The actual invitation—which I had apparently never actually read—sat in one of sixteen piles of papers on my upstairs office desk. By the time I found it, it would be too late for the party.

Through wet streets I drove the upside-down reflection of my car back home. After rasping out an explanation, I told Linda, "I don't want anything. I don't want any dinner. I just want to go to bed." I trudged upstairs to the spare bedroom feeling sorrier for myself than usual.

CURLED INTO A BALL under the covers, I wondered why tiny things tortured me, but this condition wasn't a recent development. Over the years I had attempted to balance the emotional teeter-totter with prescription drugs. The best pills only took the edge off the anxiety, while the worst ones produced bones-poking-through-my-skin side effects. I had tried meditating but kept falling asleep. Eventually I had come to accept the fact that I was a ridiculous individual.

As I endured my dark hour of the walleye, Moobie hopped up out of the shadows to keep me company. She had proven to be a faithful companion in times of trouble. On the rare occasions when I broke down in tears over some traumatic event — such as discovering a hole in my sock — Moobie materialized at my side.

She snuggled up against my leg just out of reach of my fingertips. The first few times she had done this, I had written it off as a fluke and sat up to pet her — provoking her to slip away. But her fondness for my shin was so consistent that I realized she deliberately chose the spot in order to snooze unmolested.

I used a trick to lure her closer. Pulling the blanket over my head, I lay as motionless as a frozen walleye until she ambled up and tapped my shoulder with a paw. This wasn't a request to be petted. It was a test — and I studiously ignored her. Were I to slide my arm out to stroke her, she would migrate back to my lower leg, so I pretended to be asleep. After a few moments of tapping, Moobie flopped down beside my chest and purred off into dreamland.

Suffering with a cat was always better than suffering without one. The warmth of her body, the rhythm of her breathing, and her sheer physicality provided me with a nice solid anchor in a world that seemed less real than my overreactions to it. I tried imagining the balm of two love sponges clamped against me in sweet unconsciousness—Moobie on my left, and in another twenty-four hours, Lucy on my right. How lovely to be a cat, I thought, and seldom have to think about a thing.

THE NEXT MORNING, I raced Moobie to the bathroom. Despite her advanced age, she easily outpaced me. I found her up on the toilet waiting for her water dish. We had started referring to Moobie as "I Want" due to her constant demands for one thing or another—and if the one thing wasn't water, another was. Had she been genuinely thirsty twenty-four hours a day, we might have been concerned. But she was less interested in lapping up her water than in having me serve her by holding her bowl.

I stood beside her like a sommelier with the dish for her to sample. She dipped a tentative tongue into the front, evaluated the liquid with the fussiness of a wine expert, then leaned forward to harvest the superior ambrosia in the back of the bowl.

"I can't go into work today," I told Linda as I held the bowl steady. "Not after last night."

I had started holding Moobie's water dish to try to discourage the aging cat from jumping up to the bathroom vanity. I didn't want her to break a leg at the dismount. Despite her arthritis, she still managed the occasional gazelle leap without mishap, but her surest vaults were long behind her. I would discover some months later that this practice was even more dangerous than I had imagined.

"That wasn't anything," Linda said from the bed. "Just tell them what happened."

"I'll never hear the end of it. I'll walk out into the warehouse, and Randy will say, 'Find your way up here all right? I can probably find you a GPS to borrow.' If I stay home, everyone will think I was sick."

When Moobie wasn't obsessed with water, she was begging for canned cat food. Sometimes she couldn't make up her mind which of the two she preferred. Intercepting me in the hallway, she might veer to the right into the bathroom—or she might swerve to the left into the dining room and onto another decision fork. Should she plant herself in front of the refrigerator angling for a treat, or should she amble toward the side door to go outside, eat grass, and throw up?

"What if someone asks why you weren't there?"

I hadn't thought things out that far. "I guess I'll make something up."

"You can't do that. It wouldn't be right."

"Maybe I can say I had a nosebleed that lasted all night."

Linda's silence indicated her disapproval.

Suddenly bored with the water bowl, Moobie headed for the refrigerator, intent upon back-to-back treats. I followed, but she turned on her kitty heels, trotted back into the bathroom, and requested another session with the water bowl. I wondered how she could turn such modest pleasures into the high points of her day.

But I hadn't yet met Lucy, who would flourish without a single overt joy in her life, although biting us probably came close.

I STRAGGLED INTO WORK, bracing myself for the inevitable peppering of questions and keeping the nosebleed excuse tucked in the front part of my brain. But to my immense relief, nobody mentioned the party. Everyone was too busy with the Christmas rush, so I hadn't had to make anything up.

Shortly before dinner Dave arrived at our house with Lucy in an undersize pet carrier that exaggerated her enormousness. As Lucy's massive face peered at me through the grate, I felt like Jack after having climbed the beanstalk. Surely the first time she stood up straight, she would uproot our house and carry it around on her back. The illusion of monumental proportions lessened once Dave ejected her from the carrier, and she nervously sniffed our sectional couch. But it returned when he pulled her food dish from a plastic bag. The purple

dish was far too tiny even for our dwarf rabbit, Rudy, and
it probably would have starved our parakeets. I wondered
how she had attained her ample girth as I pictured her wedg-
ing her tongue into the bowl to extract the single kibble that
would fill it to the brim.

While I crouched down to let Lucy sniff my hand, Dave
reached into the bag a second time and whisked out a litter
box that was approximately one-third the length of his cat. I
briefly considered using it as her food dish, since it appeared
brand-spanking-new. Weeks later, I would learn from Dave
that Lucy never used this or any other pet store litter box. By
that time, I had learned from personal experience that Lucy
and basic toilet hygiene didn't coexist.

"She's got a brush, too," he told me, and I strained my eyes
as he extracted the microscopic object from his jacket pocket.
"Brush her a few times, and she'll be your friend for life."

"Do you do it one hair at a time?"

"Oh, she loves being brushed. Don't you, Lucy?" She
looked glum as he poked a flap of fat that hung down from
her stomach. I vowed then I'd never tease her and earn that
grim expression—squinty eyes, flattened ears, and puffed up
cheeks—but this turned out to be her usual face.

Despite the initial unfriendliness you would expect from
any new cat, she seemed promising as a companion from the
standpoint of sheer bulk. We needed a big fat huggable cat.
Once upon a time, Moobie had filled the bill. But she had
shrunken with age, turning from a walking ottoman into a

tottering doll pillow. I thought about giving Lucy a welcoming squeeze, then changed my mind when she tried to wriggle back into her cat carrier. I wasn't sure I could have gotten my arms all the way around her, anyway.

Affecting a hunched-down armadillo posture, she scuttled upstairs. I found her under the bed, her camouflaging earth tones betrayed by a sullen stare.

Back downstairs, I told Dave, "I don't think she likes it here."

He lit up in a laugh. "She hid for two weeks when we first got her."

"It's hard for a cat to get used to a new environment."

He laughed again. "She's just being Lucy."

"Did you go to the Christmas party?" I asked.

"Hell, no. I hate those things. I'm assuming you didn't go."

"No, no, no." I waved my hand.

Moobie stood at the bottom of the stairs gazing up as if contemplating an ascent, but she turned around and ambled back into our bedroom, where visitor-shy Agnes was probably lurking. "Not to change the subject," I said, "but did you ever have a nosebleed that lasted all night."

"Not last night. Last night I had to rush Christy to the emergency room, because she forgot to take her potassium again. She couldn't unclench her hands." He balled up his fists and grimaced like a boxer. "They stuck an IV in her and made her breathe into a bag. That's why I wasn't at work today. We were up most of the night. It's the second time this has happened in two months."

"And it actually happened."

"Boy, it sure did."

Now *that* was an excuse, I thought.

As Dave was leaving, I paused at the bottom of the stairs and listened for a sign of activity from on high. "If things don't work out with Lucy," I said, "and she doesn't get along with the other cats, or she never comes out from under the bed, we may have to give her back to you."

Dave nodded. "Oh, sure."

But he knew as well as I did that we were stuck with Lucy now.

My job was more harried than usual the next day as I churned out a last-minute Christmas sale newsletter. I managed to finish and fling myself out the door before the clock finished striking noon. Back home, Moobie stared at me from the welcome mat as if she had been there the entire morning. Before she could steer me into the bathroom or the kitchen, I sidestepped her and headed for Linda's study.

She was seated on an orthopedic cushion paging through one of several knickknack catalogs scattered across her desk. "Do you think Jack would like this frog that croaks at you when you walk past it?"

"I'm sure he would." My brother-in-law loved things like that.

"You don't think it's stupid? I never know what to buy anybody."

I went upstairs to check on Lucy, who remained under the bed until I filled her bowl for the second time that morning. When she finally straggled downstairs shortly before dinner, Moobie took a wide detour into the bedroom closet, while Agnes made a snarling feint in her general direction before retreating to the basement.

I searched for a way to approach the subject gently. "Have you been petting her?" I asked Linda. "When I bent down to rub her ears a little while ago—well, it seemed like she kind of nipped me. But I might have just bumped my hand on one of the bed springs."

"She bit me this morning out of the blue."

We must have been misreading the situation. Lucy was simply suffering from a bout of unease in an unfamiliar house. Surely a cat that we had saved from the animal shelter—especially a cat that Dave had described as "very affectionate"—couldn't wait to shower us with gratitude. I told myself that it would be just a couple of more days until Lucy's love for her new owners started to flow.

CHAPTER 3

Out in the Sticks

Dinner was even more harried than usual. Bella decided to squawk instead of eat, Dusty methodically transferred his veggies into his water bowl, and I had to dash outside to figure out what was upsetting the geese. After we finally covered the cages for the night, I assumed that the drama had ended. But a theatrical sigh from Linda indicated otherwise.

"What's this?" she asked, bending down near the litter box. She touched her finger to a circle of liquid on the linoleum, raised the finger to her nose, and grimaced. "Which ungrateful cat peed on the floor again?" she asked Lucy.

"I bought the biggest litter box I could find this time."

"You'll have to get a bigger one."

"They don't make them any bigger," I said. "It's for pet

bison. It holds three hundred pounds of litter. That ought to be big enough."

Lucy had long ago gotten over her initial uneasiness to disperse her bad disposition throughout our house. In the beginning, she distributed her impressive bulk across the floor smack-dab in the middle of the highest traffic spot she could find, forcing humans, animals, and cross-country buses into a wide detour. After Christmas, she transferred the load to the dining room chair near the front door. Taking over this humble seat of oak, she had turned it into her throne. No one could pass without being subjected to her withering judgment and the frequent slap of a front paw.

"We're talking about you, Lucy Caboosey," I said.

She was awake and in what passed as a good mood when I approached her chair. She rolled onto her side, curling her paws demurely and letting her eyelids sag in a seductive invitation to pet the lovable kitty's chest. I grabbed a hind foot instead, rolling her completely over on her back, where she balanced like a beetle that had tumbled off a downspout. She held completely still in that position, purring with half-open mouth, ecstatic that I had eased her into her favorite posture for striking out with her fangs.

"Why do you want to fight with the people who love you?" The trick was letting go of her foot and jerking away my hand before the snap of her alligator jaws caught me. I won for once, though I counted my fingers to make sure.

She hadn't turned out to be the bright addition to our

household that I had expected. She reminded me of the Yakitty Yob toy robot that I had begged my parents to buy me for Christmas as a child. By sticking an arm into Yakkity's back and working the levers, you could make his eyes roll, arms open and close, and mouth move. I figured he would add much-needed color to my anemic personality. But I enjoyed my sky-blue plastic companion for barely a week.

"You got what?" Alan Jaglowski asked me during fourth-grade recess. "That's for babies. Tarte plays with baby toys!"

For the next several months, Yakitty Yob gathered dust on my bedroom shelf as a nagging reminder of my bad judgment. My mother would catch me staring glumly into space in my rehearsal for adult depression. "If you're bored, why don't you play with that Yob doll you wanted so much?" she'd say.

Linda's growing disappointment with Lucy not only pricked my guilt over having lobbied for the cat, but it also poked this ancient psychological boil.

"She thinks that as long as she stands in the litter box, she's using the litter box. She backs up all the way with her rear end hanging out into space. Do you suppose she's doing it on purpose?"

"I don't know," I said. "I don't know how she thinks."

If she was missing her litter on purpose, and there wasn't a medical reason behind the behavior, it could mean she was unhappy about her living situation. On the whole, she seemed as content as any cat that slept twenty-two hours of the day. But during her waking moments she had never approached either of us with anything resembling affection, and that struck me as odd.

"You're not paying the rent," I told Lucy, wagging a finger at her face from a safe distance.

"Paying the rent" was how our cats justified staying beneath our roof. Agnes paid the rent with the currency of cuteness. Occasionally, she tossed us the gratuity of letting us pet her and by tagging along when we took walks down to the river. She also snagged the occasional basement mouse. Moobie paid her rent by dint of having one green eye and one blue eye, which I found alternately charming and disquieting. She socked away pillowcases full of rent credit by snoozing next to me, waking from a sound sleep and switching on the purr machine, and by showering us with the coinage of her sweet personality.

Although Lucy's large round face verged on pretty, she rewarded my praises with a sucking-on-a-lemon look. In her favor, she had come to us with a pretty pink collar, and as far as I knew, her fangs didn't carry venom. But the list of negatives was longer. She wasn't nice. She had stolen a chair. She didn't like us or our other cats. She barely tolerated the touch of a hand unless her teeth got in the act. And she loved the Tom DeLay episodes of *Dancing with the Stars*. In short, she was a cat who didn't even come close to paying the rent, and her litter box misses had put her even more in arrears.

"I'll call Dave tomorrow afternoon and see if he had the same problem with her."

"And make him take her back."

"Okay," I said halfheartedly, but I had already made a promise to myself. I would do everything within my power to make Lucy like me. And if I couldn't get her to like me, I would do the next best thing: I'd outsmart her in the litter box department.

DAVE NO LONGER sat across from me each morning at work. I would have been surprised if he had, since he had taken a new job on the other end of town—a more interesting position that paid better, he claimed. But I knew this was an excuse. The real reason he had quit his job was because he couldn't bear to face me after inflicting a fat nippy nuisance of a cat on us.

"She's doing great. Everything's just fine," I told him on the phone in a voice dripping with sarcasm. I had just finishing wiping the floor behind Lucy's box before Linda could discover the latest mishap. "We don't even mind that she bites us at every possible opportunity."

"She can be a real queen bitch, that's for sure," he said, laughing—and I assumed that the term *queen bitch* was a euphemism for "very affectionate."

I described Lucy's toilet troubles. "Oh," he said, "We didn't use the litter box I brought you. We used a big plastic box that our Christmas wrapping paper came in. Even then, she overshot it. It didn't matter much, since her box was in the basement."

Reasonable people like Dave would hide a litter box in the cellar or tuck it into a corner of the bathroom. But Moobie was too arthritic to trek down a flight of stairs, and we reserved the only open corner of our bathroom for our feet. So by default I had placed the box on the open corridor that ran along one side of the living room. On the other side of the room where carpet and less sound judgment lay, we put a second litter box for the rabbits on top of an array of plastic carpet runners. At least Lucy had stayed away from the bunny box so far.

"Any chance your dad still might take her?" When Dave answered no, I experienced a twitch of relief. If we got rid of Lucy before I could get her to like me, I would feel like I had failed. And to some degree I might even miss her, which seemed to speak well for the cat. On the other hand, I had suffered a pang of regret after sweeping Yakkity Yob off my bedroom shelf and cramming him into a drawer. That feeling had quickly passed.

"What did he say?" Linda asked after I hung up.

"He misses Lucy. He wants to stop by sometime just to hang out with her."

"Good grief."

I couldn't imagine what hanging out with Lucy would entail, unless it involved a bandage and a mop. Dave obviously appreciated a side to her that I hadn't yet seen. The planetary sphere of cat lay on her back with her legs sticking straight up in the air, ready to box or bite even while fast asleep. If that continent of crabbiness possessed a temperate region, it would take a team of explorers to find it.

CHRISTMAS WAS LONG gone by now—as far in the past as dry hallway linoleum—and I knew I wouldn't find a carton of wrapping paper at the store. Even if I did, I'd end up gift wrapping Lucy and plopping her onto a stranger's porch. The thing to do instead was grab the widest, longest utility tub available, low enough for Moobie to hop into, but high enough to safely wall-in Lucy.

I reached this conclusion while sitting on the floor with my back pressed against Lucy's chair. Some cats that balked at being petted still enjoyed human company, so I was treating her to mine. Three minutes ought to be about enough, I estimated. After less than twenty seconds I realized that leaning unprotected flesh in the proximity of her mouth was dumb. I scrunched around sideways to find her studying me. I had clearly moved just in time. We glared at each other for a while. I didn't feel the love, but I wasn't giving up. I began babbling about what a good, good girl she was, and how I had never seen anything more attractive than her gray foot with a cream-colored stripe across one fat toe. She wasn't having it, however. She clunked down to the floor and headed for Moobie's kibbles as Linda walked in from outdoors.

"I'm sick of being in this house," she said.

I thought of pointing out the irony of her statement.

"I hate this house," she said in case I had missed the point the first time.

It wasn't the house that she hated as much as a winter that refused to throw in the shovel in late March. How could a woman whose lifeblood came from the sun-warmed Tennessee hills be expected to put up with it? Her relatives in Hanging Limb were at that moment filling their lungs with the scent of flowering trees as bumblebees bumped along unmowed lawns and Nashville warblers twittered from spirea bushes. While the frigid temperatures barely fazed her, the clouds drove her nuts. It could be zero degrees Kelvin outdoors, but as long as the sun shone, Linda's mood stayed bright. But a Michigan winter could go weeks without revealing a patch of blue sky.

As Linda yanked off her leaky boots, Lucy defied gravity and vaulted up onto the entertainment center. She wasn't athletic—she seemed more mineral than mammal—so to witness her leaping to the top of a three-foot-tall structure in a single bound made me realize anything was possible. It brought to mind the old adage "when pigs fly." Lying on her side, she displayed a light-brown stomach that was so large, it looked as if a second cat was nestling against her.

"Why don't you come to the store with me?" I said. "The produce section is lovely this time of year. You could buy more carrots."

Two nights earlier, I had asked at dinner, "Are these carrots all right? They're sort of whitish."

"They were getting too old for the bunnies, so I thought we'd better eat them."

I had struggled with her logic as I examined my potatoes. "The carrots aren't good enough for your rabbits, but they're good enough for your husband. What about my water? Did it come from Moobie's bowl?"

Recalling the carrots didn't improve Linda's mood. "I've got them on my list."

Lucy hopped down from the entertainment center, this time using my hi-fi speaker as a stepping stone and sending it crashing into the wall. "So much for high fidelity."

The anticipation of afternoon duck chores may have amplified Linda's glumness. We suffered more from cold-weather exposure than the mailman, newspaper carrier, and rose-bushes combined. When we weren't chipping ice out of wading pools and dragging a hose outdoors to refill them, we were knocking icicles off sagging pen-top netting and struggling to free barn doors from the grip of the frozen ground.

While I despised exertion of any description, Linda loved working outdoors in the sunshine. Her favorite job was tending her countless gardens. Worsening back problems had forced her to tinker in them by proxy. She hired helpers for the down and dirty work. But she pulled her weight not only by directing each step of the process but also by maintaining a steady stream of chatter. Keeping the conversation going with Linda was nearly as important to the job as horticultural savvy, and woe unto the helper who lacked the jaw muscles to keep up.

I knew that gardening would improve her state of mind. But it was way too early to think about the gardens yet, even if I was ready to pitch Lucy out into last year's rhubarb.

I DROVE TO the store up the street, parked my car, avoided greeting the greeter, threaded through ladies' undies, and arrived in the whereabouts of housewares barely realizing that I had made the journey. I had moved on from my preoccupation with Lucy to obsessing about Linda. When bad things happened, such as illness or pet injury, she rarely lost her head, while I rarely got out of mine. She was my rock, my support, my rock collector, my knickknack hoarder, my tofu braiser, my pet pamperer, and I couldn't stand seeing her upset. Although I couldn't bring out the sun for her, I could bring home a better litter box. I owed it to her. At least I owed it to the floor.

In the utility tub section, I discovered a daunting variety of tub widths, heights, and depths. I needed to set one in the aisle and walk around it in an approximate Lucy frame of mind, while staying upright to avoid arrest. But my access to the tubs was thwarted. The Aisle Blockers were out in full force. These were members of a secret organization whose mission was keeping shoppers away from the items they wanted to buy. Usually the Aisle Blockers operated alone. Sometimes they worked in pairs. Once during the holidays, I had witnessed a phalanx of five masterfully clogging up the store entrance.

In front of the tubs, two carts walled off the litter box–size containers. Next to the carts, two women stood chatting, completing the barricade. "Excuse me," I said, taking a step toward the tubs, but the Aisle Blockers didn't even glance at me. "I just need to get over here. Only for a second." Failing to get a response, I touched one of the carts, hoping to roll it backward ever so slightly. Without interrupting her monologue, the Aisle Blocker hooked her fingers on the cart, preventing me from budging it.

I trudged off to the pet department and spent several moments gazing longingly at the covered litter boxes, which Dave had assured me Lucy would never use. Even though she would readily enter a brown paper bag that he would leave out for her on the floor, the privacy of a covered toilet was out of the question. It was probably just as well. Even the largest model appeared too compact for Lucy's generous proportions.

By the time I returned to housewares, the Aisle Blockers had rolled off in search of fresh prey. I picked out a roomy utility tub with shallow sides and decided to bring home a toy for Lucy. A fishing pole–type gizmo with a springy wire looked promising until I noticed that the lure at the end consisted of two large feathers. Training Lucy to attack a birdlike object when we had several examples of the real thing in our dining room just felt like a bad idea. I chose a pickle-size, catnip-filled stuffed mouse instead and was about to toss it into the shopping cart, when I made a closer inspection of the rodent's attractive brown-and-black-streaked fur. It looked a little too much like our rabbit Rudy's coat because it was made from rabbit fur. I searched for an alternative, hoping I didn't run into a toy shaped like my hand.

I found a wooden stick with a small plush squid on the end and stood quietly for a minute, taking inventory of our pets. Nope, no squid. This one was definitely safe. Even better, it was downright attractive. The fuzzy tentacles tickled the hair on my arms and sent pleasant chills throbbing through my body when I dangled it against my skin. I couldn't keep my fingers off it and hoped that the security camera wasn't focused on me. I had to have it. I plucked a rabbit fur–free mousie off the shelf so that Lucy would have something to play with, too.

I BUMPED THROUGH the front door with the utility tub, hoping that the new litter box would improve Linda's mood. I heard squeals emanating from her study.

"Sweetie, one of my pen pals sent me a flier from a nursery. They've got every type of tree I've ever wanted, and they're not even expensive." I knew this to be a relative term, but next to a photo of a tiny humanoid presumably named Smithy who was dwarfed by a monstrously spreading chestnut tree, a diminutive price beckoned. "You can hardly buy a flat of impatiens for that. And they've got hydrangea, peach trees, cherry trees, flowering dogwood . . ."

"Good, good, good," I nodded to a litany of plants, trees, and shrubs, grateful for the change in indoor climate as I backed out of the room.

"And listen to this," she said, while I was still within earshot. "They're located in Tennessee. They might know some of my relatives. I can't wait to call and talk to them."

While I was happy that she had scored a shot of artificial sunlight, I wondered where she would possibly plant any of it. Thanks to our proximity to the river, two-thirds of our property was underwater each spring, so that only left the mowed confines of the yard. I was fine with walling us away from the rest of the world, but I still hoped to be able to walk out to my car without having to hack through the foliage.

I replaced Lucy's litter box with the brand new tub. Then, I freed the mousie toy from its protective packaging and with a look of wild excitement on my face vigorously shook the toy a few inches from Lucy's head. "What's this?" I asked her. "What's this?" She lifted her head up. "Get it," I hollered, "get that thing!" and flung it across the room so that it clattered against the opposite wall.

I had succeeded in capturing her interest. But it wasn't the mouse that fascinated her. The manner in which she stared at me suggested that in all of her years living with Dave and in her few months with us, she had never witnessed any behavior so absolutely and utterly foolish. Nothing even close.

I gave the other toy a halfhearted try, bouncing it up and down and dangling the tentacles in front of her face. I pretended to be undaunted by her rejection, but I wasn't squidding anyone.

ALTHOUGH THE NEXT day didn't get off to a promising start, Linda's good humor held steady. It was an overcast Saturday, and as I trudged inside from morning animal chores I heard a tussle in the kitchen. An overturned can lay on the linoleum at the base of the refrigerator. The pressure-fit plastic lid, which hadn't withstood the pressure of impact, had rolled under parrot Bella's cage. With hearing finely tuned to recognize the distinctive characteristics of tuna-packed-in-oil slopping across the floor, Lucy had materialized to lap up the chemical spill.

"How did you get in here with the door closed?" Linda said to her.

"I guess I let her in before I went outdoors." It was my latest ploy to get Lucy to like me. Snoozing under the dining room table was her latest gesture of defiance toward house rules, and I was helping her get away with it. "She doesn't even look at the birds."

"The other cats might, and when she gets in, Moobie and Agnes think they have a right to be in, too. I can't tell you how many times I've already shut this door. And since when are the cats eating tuna?"

"It's just an experiment," I said. I had been hiding the tuna can in the basement refrigerator but must have slipped and put it upstairs with the regular cat food instead. Although Linda had the reputation of being the softie when it came to animals, I was the one who spoiled the cats. I figured that bad behavior would go away if I just made a cat a little bit happier, even though years of keeping cats hadn't produced a shred of evidence that this was true.

"I couldn't keep her out of here yesterday," she said. "I'd chase her out, and she would scuttle away making this teeny, tiny little 'mew' as if I had offended her, but she doesn't stay offended like other cats. Two minutes later, she comes marching right back in again, as if she's got every right to be there. She doesn't even try to sneak. She comes barreling right in. *Hi, here I am.*"

As Linda nudged Lucy out from under the table with her foot, Agnes darted up from the basement stairs for an impromptu fight. I carried the squirming black cat into the living room and set her on the couch. The basement and/or dining room door opened and/or closed just long enough for Lucy's unceremonious ejection. She certainly wasn't doing anything to advance her standing with Linda.

Meanwhile, my utility tub litter box failed the acid test. "She's still too big," said Linda, scrunching up her nose. Just to confirm the identity of the acrid liquid on the floor, she dipped a finger and gave the substance a sniff. Linda had never been squeamish about close interaction with whatever interested her. Once before we were married and were looking at houses, a realtor had been unlocking the door of one that we were about to tour when Linda picked up a stone. Wondering what it might look like when wet, she had licked it.

The utility tub wasn't small. If it were any larger, we would have to build a footbridge over it. Clearly the matter required a fresh approach. Returning to the store up the street, I bought a second utility tub exactly like the first one. I cut out the bottom, cut out an opening in the front, and bolted it upside down on top of the original tub to form a perimeter wall that was now twice as high. It would keep the floor dry as long as Lucy didn't stand with her rear end oriented exactly toward the opening after she had stepped inside. I didn't regard the upside-down tub's lip as significant, but I would learn otherwise.

As I was performing tub surgery in the basement, I heard Linda merrily chatting on the phone upstairs. I could usually guess from the subject matter which one of her friends was on the other end, but the broad range of topics from pets to favorite vegetarian recipes stumped me.

"Who was that?" I asked, once I had set up the improved litter box and coaxed a few syllables of faint praise from Linda.

"I met the nicest woman at the Tennessee nursery. She sounded like a grandma lady. The postage is the same no matter how many things you order! The postage is still four dollars. *Four dollars.* She didn't know any of my relatives, but she has three cats, and she loves the Lord. One of her sons is over there in Iraq."

I shouldn't have been surprised. Linda held extended conversations with the greeters at the store down the street and knew each of them by name. These were the same women who would bid me "Have a nice day" as I was walking out the door and then snap their heads away so sharply to avoid my reply that I wished I owned a piece of the local chiropractic practice.

"They won't ship until the weather is warmer up here. About three weeks, she said."

I gave Lucy's new litter box a proud inspection, satisfied that I had been true to my vow. Although I hadn't succeeded in coaxing even the smallest gesture of affection from her, I had kept the other half of my bargain with myself. Surely I had finally solved our hallway "bathroom" problems.

IN THE WEEKS that followed, nobody appreciated the warming weather more than Agnes. She spent every moment outdoors worrying rodents and rolling in the weeds. Even though she lacked front claws, she pursued the squirrels up saplings, dozed in the elbow of our redbud tree, and perched on top of a fence post and glared into the dining room at dinner. This last stunt impressed me. It implied a thought process superior to ordinary begging, which merely involved parking herself in front of a person with food. Her fence-topping behavior meant: *my sitting in this unusual spot has a meaning for you that is different from my sitting anywhere else.*

To usher in the start of spring, Linda set out a pair of

hummingbird feeders and brewed a quart jar of sun tea on top of the picnic table. I hadn't realized that a connection existed between the hummingbird feeders and the sun tea until I caught Linda making me a glass of tea. "It's best when it's sweet," she said. She tossed in the ice cubes, then sloshed in a shot of hummingbird nectar.

"It's just sugar water," she told me as my eyes popped open.

"Is this the sugar water the hummingbirds are getting, or is it the sugar water that isn't good enough for the hummingbirds?"

When I buzzed into the living room with my ice tea clutched beneath one wing, I noticed Lucy huddled inside the clothes basket on top of our clean laundry. Recalling Dave's comment that she loved to ride around on things, I dragged the basket across the rug. She hunkered down as if preparing to leap out, one ear cocked forward and the other folded back. Even though she was poised for action, her low center of gravity made her look less like a cat than a cast-iron tortoise. And she remained in her crouching posture as I lugged the basket in the opposite direction. But spinning it was probably too much of a good thing. Round about the second revolution, she tumbled out, indicating offense by licking a hind leg before assuming her seat of judgment on the wooden chair. I couldn't claim to have delighted her, but the fact that she had tolerated a brief attempt at playfulness gave me grounds for hope.

On my way upstairs to check my e-mail, I scanned the floor behind the litter box and was pleased to find it dry.

Then I investigated more closely. Somehow the narrow rim of the upside-down utility tub that I had bolted to the right-side-up one—a channel no wider than a third of an inch at most—was filled with liquid. Yet she hadn't spilled a drop on the linoleum. Drawing upon incredible natural talent, Lucy had achieved the feline equivalent of Annie Oakley shooting the pip out of an ace of spades while astride a pair of stallions.

I called Linda into the room to show her this once-in-a-lifetime, never-to-be-witnessed-again feat. "That's the second time she's done that this week," she said.

LINDA WAITED EVERY morning for an overloaded UPS truck, but I had completely forgotten about her pending shipment of landscaping foliage until two weeks later when I trundled in with our mail in one hand and two bags of lettuce for the ducks in the other. "My trees and bushes came," she said. "Did you see that little tube?"

"I haven't had time to see anything."

"That cardboard tube—about twice as fat as a Christmas wrapping paper tube."

Following her finger, I noted a flattened cardboard cylinder on the floor with shoe prints on one end as if it had been ground under a heel. "That's one sorry tube," I said as I took a step toward the living room to snatch the binoculars from my dresser drawer. I had just heard the *zee-zee-zee-zoe-zee* of a black-throated green warbler and wanted to ogle it before it moved on. But Linda blocked my path.

"That dinky little thing is what all my trees and bushes came in."

"How many tubes were there?" Only half listening, I considered ducking under her arm and slipping past. We rarely got a single warbler all by its lonesome during spring migration, and I was chomping at the bit to discover who else was in the yard.

"One tube. There's only one. My trees and bushes are nothing but these." She held up a stick too miserable to make a decent parakeet perch. "This one says 'hydrangea.' Another one that looks identical or maybe even worse claims to be my peach tree, if you can even read the label. They've probably got a little office, and when you call in and place an order, they count out some wet twigs from a vat, write out tags, and ship them to some poor unsuspecting person who was expecting beautiful plants."

"Will that thing even grow?"

"If you've got fifteen years." At the base of the stick she tweaked a tiny vegetative beard swaddled in plastic wrap. "It's called bare root. The lady on the phone claims that the circular clearly states that all the plants they ship are bare root."

"What happened to your 'grandma lady'?" I made another feeble effort to slide by.

"This was somebody mean sounding who said I should have read the fine print."

"I'd send them back."

"I can't. If any of them don't grow, I can return them, but

they won't refund my money. All they'll do is send me another stick."

"I don't remember seeing any note about bare roots, and I'm sure you would have noticed it, if there was one."

"You probably need a microscope to read the dumb thing."

"Do you still have the flyer?" I followed Linda into her study and turned the brochure inside and out. But there wasn't so much as a mustard seed of a reference to the exchange of cash for soggy twigs. "Granny lied to you," I said.

Finally at long last making it to my dresser to grab the binoculars, I was primed to find the black-throated green warbler when Lucy's glum expression slowed me down. She had somehow managed to implicate the dining room chair in her bad mood, and I could sense invisible particles of unhappiness streaming toward me. Suddenly I felt guilty that she had never manifested the slightest glimmer of pleasure in our house. Any other cat would have rolled around in glee at causing her owners the amount of trouble that she had inflicted upon us, but to all appearances we were suffering in vain. "Sweetie, what more can I do for you?" I asked.

In the great scheme of things—measured against a backdrop of war, pestilence, or other cats, for example—she wasn't so terrible. Moobie and Agnes were hardly paragons of good behavior. Moobie had very occasionally mistaken our bedroom rug for the litter box, and 99 percent of Agnes' affectionate outpourings were manipulations in the service of scoring a treat. In her favor, Lucy was rarely underfoot, had yet to set a paw upon the basement stairs, and would never consider expending her limited energy reserves by hopping up onto the bathroom vanity for water. She was extremely economical in her begging, too, demanding food with a single curt meow and a wobbling march toward her bowl.

"You're okay," I told her before breaking outdoors into the sunshine, and she was. Apart from the biting, the surliness, the lack of affection for us, the disdain for our other cats, the chair thievery, the bold incursions into the dining room, and the lousy bathroom hygiene, she was just this side of perfect.

ALONG THE RIVER from the crowns of maples and from leafless thickets I was excited to hear unfamiliar songs. But every bird that I caught in my binoculars turned out to be nothing more exotic than a chickadee, titmouse, or goldfinch, and I swore that some of them were smirking at me.

My neck hurt from supporting my foolish head in a variety of awkward positions, and my back hurt from hauling two fifty-pound bags of poultry feed out to the barn. I took a hot shower and eased down flat on my back on the living room floor in front of the so-called entertainment center.

I felt a house-shaking thud and then the play of paws in my wet hair. I had already let Agnes outdoors to harass chipmunks, and Moobie was snoozing on the bed. That only left Lucy. I made a courageous leap of faith. I reached behind my head to pet her, although chances were excellent that she would bite me. But I didn't want to turn around and risk spoiling our first moment of shared affection. No nip came as I rubbed the fur around her collar. In fact, as I scratched her neck, she licked my forehead and purred, pushing her face into my hair.

"You're not any trouble," I said. "You're just being Lucy."

My efforts forcing her to like me hadn't gotten me anywhere. I didn't need to sit with my back against her chair and garland her with praises. I didn't need to pet her when she wasn't in the mood, shake a mousie toy next to her ear, or drag her around in a laundry basket, either. I didn't need to bribe her with tuna or let her hide beneath the dining room table. As it turned out, all I had to do to win her heart was to scent my hair with pine tar–based antidandruff shampoo.

This event turned into a daily routine. I'd take a shower after dinner, and with a clipped "mew" Lucy would call me on the carpet, commanding me to lie down on the floor for her evening aromatherapy and neck massage. When she grew tired of inhaling my hair, she would stroll down to my opposite pole, flopping down perpendicular to my feet and hooking a front paw around my ankle. I was expected to stay prone until it suited her to leave. If this wasn't love on her part, at least it passed for a positive interaction.

CHAPTER 4

....

Fred Mertz Meets the Mummy

Although I had gotten Lucy to like me by happenstance rather than by design, I still considered it to be a triumph of my coddling her versus Linda's commonsense approach. But even a moist-eyed sentimentalist like me would think twice about taking in another cat after living with Lucy, so it was fortunate that Frannie's arrival on our porch was still months away. As Halloween crept up on us, another cat calamity was beginning to unfold. This time I thought I could stave off disaster by outsmarting one of our cats, though I should have known better.

The trouble started small, as trouble often does. It started small and red.

It started as I wrestled with a bundle of corn shocks that were heavier than I was. They threw me to the ground a few times as I struggled to tie them to a tree. Before that, I had

hung a stuffed ghost from the branches and found a light bulb
for the plastic pumpkin that winds walloped against our steps
each year. I didn't dislike any of these rituals so much, at least
not compared to the horrors of trying to carve a decent jack-
o'-lantern. Linda's would look like a work of art. Mine would
resemble a drawing by a blindfolded child.

I was racking my brain for a way to avoid this embarrass-
ment when a spooky red spot appeared among Linda's hostas
and drifted across the lawn.

"Moobie, you're not supposed to be outside," I told her. Our
basement door must have failed to close again and she had
gotten out.

The red spot near her right shoulder had first shown up
as a blemish a month ago. It hadn't seemed like anything at
first. But incessant licking had transformed a pinkish bump
into an angry sore that stood out against her white fur like
a bright red LED. A few years ago, our big pet rabbit Walter
had developed a tumor on his shoulder that had begun as a
small red spot. It turned out to be cancer, and it did him in. I
was already nervous about taking her to the vet the next day.

Moobie slipped through my hands as I reached down to
grab her, evading me with unexpected nimbleness considering she was now fifteen years old. Being out in the wild had
a transformational effect on the most staid and chair-bound
house cat—excepting Lucy, of course, who only lumbered
out to sleep in the sun. Moobie and Agnes changed into wild-
eyed primal creatures once they received an unfiltered jolt

of the outdoors. They became hunters, but it was more than that. The outdoors energized their contradictory impulses, making them by turns furtive and at ease, bold and awed, madly affectionate and more disdainful of people than usual. The effect was just short of supernatural, but it really was nature, pure and simple.

A lithe and fluid Moobie skimmed the ankle-deep fallen leaves as I plowed through them at her kitty heels. She passed through the fence while I fumbled with the gate, then bounded up the steps of the side door, begging to go indoors.

FEW EVENTS IN life caused me more stomach-churning trauma than driving a pet to the vet. Our animals never acted as if they appreciated the honor of a jaunt in my Ford Focus, though a goose had patrolled the backseat with flapping wings and seemed excited by the trucks that passed us on the freeway. Our most macho African grey parrot squeaked pitifully in the car, and while our rabbits never uttered a syllable of complaint, they busied their front paws scratching furiously at the carrier, trying to dig their way back home. But it was always the cats that made the biggest fuss.

Moobie howled constantly on the short trip to see our kitty vet Dr. Ziaman. No amount of wheedling, cooing, or clucking noises would reassure her. Her cries were so loud that a man in a pickup truck pulled onto the shoulder waiting for an emergency vehicle to go by. "You're okay, honey. We're almost there," I told her as I poked my fingers through the front grate

of her carrier. She rubbed her face against them and was quiet
for a few hundred yards.

Moobie and I traded psychological spaces once we were
inside the building. I was the one who wanted to howl. Waiting rooms have never failed to unnerve me, even for nothing
more life threatening than a haircut. The minutes perched
on a hard-backed chair in Dr. Ziaman's lobby ticked by with
the slowness of a glacial epoch. There were two ways to cope
with the waiting room blues. One was wearing the ink off a
magazine as I flipped back and forth through the same few
pages. The other was staring at a spot on the wall until the
rest of the room dissolved around me.

At least these particular walls provided a bit of seasonal
stimulation. Colorful cutouts depicted a black cat curling its
body around a jack-o'-lantern, whose carefree smiling face
I never could have carved. A bat flapped close by, sharing
airspace with a spider. The cardboard ghost had frightened
himself over nothing. I couldn't help noticing that he had my
weak chin and pointy nose.

I reached inside the carrier and extracted Moobie with the
idea of comforting her, though I was actually trying to comfort myself. I wanted to knead her fur between my fingers,
feel her squirm on my lap then settle down, and hear her
purr. But she refused to settle down, and the purring part was
out of the question. She thrashed her legs until I managed to
squeeze her back inside her carrier. Even as I resolved not
to worry about the red spot, an unruly chunk of my brain

decided to revisit every unhappy pet diagnosis I had ever received.

A vet tech rescued me, directing me to an examination room for another wait between frozen clock hands. Dr. Ziaman's voice in the corridor lifted my spirits. When she walked in, she lit up the examination room with so much cheerfulness, I marveled that she didn't snuff me out like a candle, leaving only a wisp of smoke where I had stood. Hopping off the counter, Moobie headed for the nearest corner of the room and compacted herself to the diameter of a saucer. She was typically unperturbed around people but distrustful of the veterinary profession. I didn't imagine that the dog yips and wall thumps from the room next door were helping to put her at ease.

"Moobs, what's going on?" she asked. "How are you, Mr. Tarte?"

Briefly but vainly hoping I'd been the "Moobs" so enthusiastically addressed, I activated Mr. Tarte's skinny arms to scoop the cat up off the floor. She suddenly didn't mind being held as an alternative to being set down on the examination table. I pointed out the red spot on her upper front leg.

"Well, it looks like cancer, but it would take a biopsy to make sure," Dr. Ziaman told me. "If it is cancer, she'll need to get it removed."

At another round of wall thumps from next door, I laid my hand on Moobie's back. "She's too old for that. She doesn't do well with anesthetics. Isn't it possible that it's just a mole or wart that's been there forever, but she's bothering it now for some reason? I'm thinking that if she left it alone for a while and it didn't get any worse, she might be okay."

"We could try that for a few days," she said, compressing more animation and positive energy into a single nod than I had dribbled into my entire life. "We could try her with an Elizabethan collar and give the ulcer a chance to heal."

"An Elizabethan collar?" I imagined the classic drawing of Shakespeare with Moob's face in place of Will's.

"It fits around her neck and sort of looks like a funnel. Some people call it the satellite dish."

I shook my head. I couldn't see putting her through the misery. "What if I tape up her leg to keep her from getting at the boo-boo?"

"I don't think you'd be able to keep a bandage on her," she said. "Cats are really good at undoing things."

I resisted telling Dr. Ziaman that I was far cleverer than any cat; it struck me as too obvious to have to say. But I could be excused my misconceptions since Moobie hadn't yet demonstrated just how clever she was.

As I ferried the white howler home, I reassured myself that Dr. Ziaman was wrong. Wrong that the little red spot was cancer, and wrong that I couldn't keep the little red spot of cancer from getting worse by taping it up.

OUT OF THE fifty-some animals that lived in our house and in two outdoor pens, we had paid money for very few.

Most had knocked on our front door, tiny cloth suitcase in hand, because they had nowhere else to go.

Moobie had been evicted from Linda's son Ben's house because he and his wife supposed that Moobie might be the trigger for their daughter's juvenile asthma. She stayed briefly with Linda's mom, who was getting too wobbly to take on a permanent pet. So I drove back from Battle Creek to Lowell with one hand on the wheel, the other hand clapped over an ear, Linda in the backseat, and wailing Moobie in the front. Before I had pulled the key out of the ignition, Linda had already penned an irresistible cat-for-adoption ad for our local weekly newspaper.

We were certain we would find Moobie a good home, which indicated our level of naiveté in the cat rescuing game. If you run a classified ad for a free parakeet, bunny, or even a pet duck, you will definitely get some calls. But if you advertise a cat, it's as if your phone service has suddenly been cut off. You've never been so lonely in your entire life. Just about the time you've given up, you'll get one, and only one, response. But the adoption is doomed to fail. Either your new best friend will turn a nose up at your cat at the last minute, or you'll realize you would rather send your kitty to the salt mines than surrender her to such a villain.

Or there may a hyperactive child involved. The woman who professed that she had always wanted a white cat with one blue eye and one green eye sounded promising on the phone. Her soft-spoken manner turned out to be a negative, though.

Moobie scooted off to hide as the woman's two-year-old girl chased her around the rocking chair in our living room while the mom clucked her tongue. The clucking escalated into a sharp expulsion of air as the tyke pursued Moobie upstairs and earned a vigorous growl from Agnes. Seconds later, as the strict nondisciplinarian comforted her sobbing child, Linda told her, "We'll get back to you"—as in, *We'll get back to you in the next life when Bob and I return as Martian colonists.*

We held out hope for a second applicant, putting out the word to everyone that we needed a home for a nice cat. Friends left to learn flamenco dancing in Spain. E-mail acquaintances abandoned their ISPs. Even telemarketers stopped calling for fear that we would ask them. When Linda ran another ad, the happy twittering of songbirds faded into stillness. The river behind our house dried to hard-baked mud. As cobwebs enveloped our front door, the unexpected happened. We fell more in love with Moobie than we did with the notion of giving her up.

She had won us over with her good nature. When I'd walk into the living room after a long absence of, say, twenty minutes, she would be so thrilled to renew my acquaintance that she couldn't constrain herself to the floor. She'd hop up to the back of our couch to increase her visibility and thus her chances of being petted. She radiated joy throughout our house.

Agnes was none too happy about her presence, though. She growled at Moobie whenever she intruded upon the ever-changing invisible boundaries that defined Agnes' territory. Moobie responded like Gandhi, refusing to retreat—especially from the feed bowl in the hall. Upon emptying the dish, she would turn herself into a pudgy cloud and airily pass by the hissing offender.

I had wanted a cat like Moobie with one green eye one blue eye all of my life, even though I hadn't known it until she arrived.

WHEN WE FIRST got Moobie, it had been hard to hold myself back from teasing her about her roly-poly architecture. "Little pink ears, little pink toes, big pink belly, little pink nose," I used to tell her as I poked her stomach. Just in time for Halloween, I needed a different kind of incantation now, a spell that would make the red spot disappear.

At the store down the street, I braved the Aisle Blockers and emerged with a roll of magical tape that stuck to itself but not to any of the other elements in the periodic table. It had to be magic, because it consisted of empty space held together by a mesh that was "flesh tone," according to the packaging, but only if you happened to be a sun-broiled Caucasian.

I placed a small gauze pad on Moobie's upper leg as she snoozed on Linda's pillow. Then I added a few windings of the magical tape, snipping it and smoothing it into place, neat as a bud on a branch. As I sat back to admire my handiwork, Moobie blinked awake, shook off her fog of slumber, and shucked off the bandage as easily as I would pull down a sock on an energetic day.

I caught her in midair as she hopped off the bed, and I shut the door with my foot. I returned her to Linda's pillow until I had fabricated a wider bandage. It was far less tidy than my initial effort, because a wide-awake Moobie squirmed a half-dozen times for every twist of the tape. When I had finished, I let her go, and she spun off like a spring that had suddenly sprung. With tooth and claw she did her best to undo my deed, but the bandage held.

"Sweetheart," I called, striding triumphantly into the dining room, where Linda was changing the parrot cage newspapers. "I've solved the problem of Moobie licking her leg."

"You have? How?"

"Come take a look." I led her into the bedroom and stood back so she could experience an unencumbered view of Moobie vigorously licking the sore on her leg with my bandage bunched around her foot like a bootie.

"We should say prayers for her," Linda suggested.

"And for me. A special prayer for patience."

"CAN WE CARVE our pumpkins after dinner?" Linda asked in a plaintive voice which indicated that I had already put her off as long as possible.

To take my mind off my troubles with Moobie, I had been busy thinking of ways to spare myself this seasonal humiliation. In the process of trying to come up with an excuse like a sudden wrist sprain, an innovative sculpting method had occurred to me.

Once we had finished eating, after Linda had mopped the floors and played with Dusty, and I had vacuumed the dining room and given Bella her night-night treat, and Linda had re-filled the birds' water dishes, and I had covered the cages, and Linda had scrubbed the countertop on which Howard the dove had eaten diced spaghetti, and I had minced chunks of chicken and fed them to the cats, Linda brought in her globu-lar pumpkin, and I fetched my elongated ovoid pumpkin.

As Linda sorted through the jar lids, twist ties, and packets of take-out food chopsticks in the silverware drawer in quest of the perfect knife, I scampered down to the basement and scurried up again with the cordless drill that I had already fitted with a one-inch spade bit. My burst of creative com-position was short and sweet. To the music of a soft electro-mechanical whirring, corkscrews of orange-colored pulp spun away and dropped onto the kitchen countertop. Before Linda had even finished sketching out her design, I had al-ready bored four holes in my pumpkin respectively represent-ing the eyes, nose, and mouth. My jack-o'-lantern done.

"That's really cool!" she said as I showed her the minimal-ist face. While my creation literally wouldn't hold a candle to the classic Norman Rockwell jack-o'-lantern that she soon brought to life, I had avoided the usual drudgery while also managing to forget about the red spot for a little while.

Riding high from my modernist breakthrough, I tried a different approach to bandaging Moobie. Using up the re-mainder of the magical tape, I swaddled the full length of her leg from her ankle up to just below her shoulder. Refusing to trust the weak molecular bond of the mystery material, I secured the top and bottom with plain old commonplace run-of-the-mill adhesive tape. When I was finished, she did her best to pull off the wrap, but she couldn't locate a loose end to unravel and had to settle for listlessly burnishing it with her tongue. I triumphantly ushered Linda into the room, and she beheld a cat stymied by human ingenuity.

"I'm sure glad the bandage worked," I told Linda by way of bragging just before we went to bed. Moobie had moved her base of slumber operation from our bed to the couch and showed no signs of struggling against the tape.

"Don't you think you should take her to Dr. Hedley for a second opinion?" He was the zoo vet who had successfully treated several of our critters.

"We don't need to," I said. "Give this a couple of days, and you'll see a tremendous change."

The next morning I was awakened by a familiar scratching at the bedroom door. We didn't need an alarm clock with Moobie in the house. She wanted water at the sink or canned cat food—or she simply wanted me up at 5:30 AM in ample time for us to share the 7:12 AM sunrise. But when I opened the bedroom door, Moobie had vanished in the gloom. She hadn't left without a trace, however. At the spot where she had been standing, she had left the leg wrap as a memento.

• • •

I NEEDED TO get away from Moobie and reconsider my strategy, which is how Linda talked me into leaving the house.

Living outside of the village limits, we received an average of zero trick-or-treaters each year, which was a lower number of costumed tikes than what it took to please Linda. If the revelers wouldn't come to us, she would find them among the Halloween decorations in town. Under the dim glow of street-lights, this gave her a chance to see kids dressed as the latest video-game entities wearing heavy winter coats.

"Should we put the rabbits back?"

"No, they're not hurting anything," I said as Frieda rubbed her chin against a chair and little round Rudy huddled disguised as a coconut. "We'll only be a few minutes." I was wrong on both counts, of course.

"OH, LOOK AT THAT HOUSE. That's an incredible decoration."

Linda, who had been lying flat on the backseat for the sake of her sacrum, sat up and glanced out the window. "That isn't a decoration, that's the gas station."

I was marginally interested in finding over-the-top Halloween bad taste to rival Christmas exhibit excess, but nobody covered their lawn with phony tombstones or projected the image of a fanged Elvis on the side of their garage, as I'd hoped. The displays were pretty low-key. Flickering orange lights and undulating air-filled jack-o'-lanterns competed with the darkened houses of holiday haters, whose total lack of décor I envied.

"We might as well give up," I said.

"Just one more neighborhood," Linda said.

Several just-one-more-neighborhoods later, my warnings about Linda's ensuing back pain allowed me to zigzag us home again. As we got out of the car, I admired the New Guinean tribal mask aesthetic of my pumpkin. But when we stepped onto the porch, we realized something was terribly wrong. "What's that smell?" asked Linda. "The living room is filled with smoke!"

"What did you do?" I demanded as I fumbled the key in the lock, visions of asphyxiated parrots dancing in my head. "Did you leave something on the stove?"

Linda barreled ahead of me, checked to make sure the parrots, parakeets, and dove were fine, then chugged back into the living room, where the white smoke was concentrated. Frieda hid behind the coffee table with her ears flat against her head. When she noticed that I noticed her, she thumped a hind foot to express her dissatisfaction and slunk out of the room at record slinking speed.

"No, I didn't leave anything on the stove," Linda said.

She propped our light-up ghost in front of the front door to hold it open. I extended a leg to block Agnes and shut her in the basement, since I didn't think a black cat ought to be running around outside on Halloween. It just seemed like bad luck. As the smoke dissipated, Linda walked stooping, braids waggling like a pair of bloodhound ears, as she sniffed her way to the cause of the combustion. "The carpet's charred over here." She went down on one knee. "And the bottom of the bookcase is burnt."

"It's the power strip," I said. "It melted."

She was almost lying on the floor. "The rug is wet right here."

"How could it be wet?" Then I remembered Frieda. Out of all the places for her to take a bathroom break, she had decided on the eight-outlet surge protector, causing a massive short. "That's the last time they're allowed out while we're gone."

"She may have started the fire," Linda said. "But she also put it out."

FRIEDA'S FIREBUGGING PLUNGED me into a foul mood that was 50 percent depression and 60 percent anxiety. The combination simultaneously drained my energy and over-stimulated me. Moobie's expertise at stepping out of any bandage I concocted didn't improve my outlook. One day too late for the holiday, I had turned into a full-blown crab.

As I trudged through the living room, I passed Linda stretched out on her usual spot on the floor atop her faux-sheepskin rug. Lucy was immune to the charms of my wife's hair and always let her lie in peace. Linda was telling the story of our near immolation to some friend or relative on the phone — or to a grandma lady employed by a shady nursery. "It could only happen to us," she said. "It's like something out of the *I Love Lucy* show."

In the bedroom I found Moobie in her usual position on the pillow and decided to wrap her as she had never been wrapped before. I ignored the magical mystery tape in favor of a brand new weapon in my bandage arsenal: a roll of plain old gauze. I wrapped her leg from elbow to shoulder, looped the gauze twice around her chest so that the legging couldn't slide off under any circumstances. Then I tied both ends tightly.

"Stop fighting me. I'm trying to save your life," I told her as she struggled to get away.

Close to morning, a pang of fear woke me. It started as a clenched feeling in my stomach, spread through my limbs, and made itself at home in my brain, where it stuck to passing thoughts like a huge refrigerator magnet. I obsessed over Moobie, Linda's back, politics, money, the cluttered upstairs, and whether I had remembered to latch the goose pen door. The worry made me weary, and I collapsed back into sleep.

The next time I lifted my head, our bed had been transported to an old-fashioned Hollywood soundstage. Propped up on pillows, Linda and I watched *I Love Lucy* on an ancient black-and-white TV. Laughing somewhat menacingly, Fred Mertz marched around the perimeter of our bed dressed in a white shirt and with his pants hitched high. I was mildly surprised to find him in the room, but I was more perplexed that Ethel wasn't with him.

"William Frawley and Vivian Vance didn't get along in real life," I told Linda in the dream. "Maybe that's why she isn't here."

This was the wrong thing to say. Throwing himself onto the mattress, an enraged Fred Mertz clutched me in a bear hug, pinning my arms and growling in my ear. I squeaked out a laugh, hoping that his foolery was part of the show, but he squeezed me harder until I could barely breathe. Finally, the iron grip loosened and I managed to work one arm free, and then the other. Rolling over, I threw him to the floor. Awake at last, I checked the time on my digital watch just to ground myself in ordinary reality.

Apparently the dream was therapeutic. As Linda slumbered on, I all but floated above the mattress in a state of bliss that an archangel would envy. Liberated from the Fred Mertz side of my personality, I felt refreshed and in my first good mood in weeks. I hadn't realized just how much tension I'd been carrying around until I had thrown it to the floor. He had been really, really scary. Leave it to my unconscious to skip over all the Hollywood monsters—Frankenstein, Dracula, Shirley Temple—only to terrorize me with a negative projection of myself.

I CHANNELED THE buoyant Lucy-Ricky side of my psyche as I toiled at the usual morning drudgery, struck by the newness of each experience in my worry-free frame of mind. I paused while emptying the dishwasher to admire the cleanliness of a fork. I spent an extra moment talking to Dusty, calling him "Mr. Bubby" and "the great big bean burrito," then asked Frieda if she'd started any fires recently.

Linda padded into the kitchen to make coffee as I diced grapes and a piece of pear for Bella. "I've decided what I want on my tombstone," I said.

"Why are you thinking about that now?"

"I'm not. But I was thinking that I want it to say, 'He could cut up fruit really small.' "

My lofty mood grew even more elevated when I turned on the bathroom spigot for Moobie and noticed that she hadn't managed to slip off her Fred Mertz of an iron-gripping bandage. I was proud of my work until she teetered on the toilet. A glance at her leg explained the reason why. I had wound the tape too tightly, cutting off the circulation. Her leg and paw had swollen to almost twice their normal size. Horrified, I scissored off the gauze and checked her over to determine if she needed to be rushed to the vet. Unconcerned, she scrambled up onto the sink, rubbed her head against my chest, and stuck her face under the faucet.

"What did I do to you, sweetheart? I'm so sorry." She didn't require an apology, though—she just required her water. Since her mobility wasn't impaired, I knew that the condition wasn't serious and the swelling would soon go away. But I still felt guilty and vowed that my bandaging days had come to an end.

Over our morning coffee, I told Linda what had happened. "You're right, she should go to Dr. Hedley," I said. If the zoo vet could give a hyena an appendectomy—which I presumed was what he did on a typical day—he could certainly help us with a sore on a cat's leg. "So now we're right back where we started, back to square one," I said. "It's like watching a rerun."

"The *I Love Lucy* show," Linda said, echoing her remark from the previous day.

But I had to disagree with her. If my life resembled a bad Hollywood production, it was something far scarier than a sitcom. "Not *Lucy*," I told her as Moobie hobbled in. "More like *The Mummy's Curse*."

. . . .

CHAPTER 5

The Funnel of Happiness

A most unwelcome sound awoke me in the morning.

Buf, buf, buf, buf, buf.

I tended to sleep so lightly that I had bought an over-size watch just for checking the time overnight without my glasses. The dial light allowed me to chronicle the exact second when the creak of a floorboard roused me. I checked it now, plunging the room into an eerie green luminescence. Just as I had suspected, it was too late to go back to sleep and too early to get up and start chopping up fruit. I wasn't eager to jump-start the day, since I would be taking the white howler to see Dr. Hedley in the afternoon.

Flump. Flump, flump, flump, flump.

It was an abrasive, disconcerting sound. If you had never

heard it before and didn't know what it meant, you'd be tempted to pry open your window and make a break for the neighbor's house. I heard the noise every morning and knew exactly what it meant, and I was still considering bolting into the woods.

Run, run, run, run, run.

I tried ignoring it. Surely if I didn't answer Moobie's summons, she would tire of beating a tattoo on the drum of our bedroom door. I hoped that Linda might get up and shoo her away, but she had once slept through a car crashing into a tree at the edge of our front yard.

Dolt, dolt, dolt, dolt, dolt.

We had tried locking Moobie in the bathroom overnight with a blanket to curl up on, but she generated a wall-piercing wail that even managed to penetrate Linda in the Land of Nod. I suggested letting her roam the basement with scads of mice to keep her company and piles of laundry for bedding. But Linda had talked me out of confining an arthritic cat to a space that turned into a cold dungeon nine months of the year. So we were serenaded with bongo solos every morning a few minutes either side of five thirty.

The accuracy of Moobie's chronometer amazed me. Whenever daylight saving time kicked in or faded out, I shunted from room to room adjusting clocks and hourglasses, but Moobie would be confused about the time change for exactly one day—the Sunday morning of the change. By Monday morning she had corrected her internal Bulova to clamor for my services at the usual time.

Come, come, come, come, come.

Instead of letting her lead me to faucet or feed dish, I decided to simply let her inside the room. In all the years that we'd had her, it was remarkable that this option had never occurred to me before. Chances were excellent that she would relish snuggling up against the boniest portion of my leg, giving me an extra twenty minutes to fantasize about life on a cat-free tropical island. It seemed that I'd succeeded as she parked herself against my shin.

The next moment she was thumping my head with her timpani-banging paws.

Time to get up.

I OFTEN WISHED I had a family physician like Dr. Hedley. He could deliver the worst news with reassurance, and his expertise was encyclopedic. He had diagnosed a microscopic skin parasite with our bunny Frieda that another vet had missed, and he had also performed delicate pancreatic surgery on my sister Joan's ferret Beethoven. Almost as appealing as his bottomless pit of knowledge was his treasure trove of tales from his decades as a zoo consultant. During routine visits when no critter's life or epidermis was at risk, he would let me steer him through an archipelago of zoological anecdotes.

But today the news about Moobie wasn't so jolly. Dr. Hedley concurred with Dr. Ziaman's diagnosis and told me that the red spot was a tumor, and that the tumor was probably malignant.

"I suggest we remove it right way," he said. After listening to her chest, he shook his head to free the stethoscope from his ears. I figured this was a technique he'd perfected when he needed both hands to subdue a wombat. "She does have a slight heart murmur, and that's cause for some concern, but the surgery should go pretty quickly. We won't have her under anesthesia any longer than we need to. And the good news is that even if the tumor is malignant, this is not a kind of cancer that typically spreads."

"It isn't?" I asked, just to hear him repeat this encouraging tidbit.

"No, it's not. Once we've removed the tumor and the incision is allowed to heal, she should make a full recovery with no recurrence of the cancer."

I fully expected Moobie's irregular heart to rhythmically fall in line during surgery. However, I suspected that her tongue would be less cooperative. "She does have a tendency to want to lick the spot."

"They become obsessed," he said. "Even when there's nothing there to lick, they'll keep on licking anyway." Right on cue, Moobie straightened up and started worrying the sore. "She'll have to wear an Elizabethan collar."

"She won't do well with that."

"She'll hate it," he said, deflating me by agreeing. "They get stuck when they're trying to go places, they bump into things, and it makes it hard for them to eat. But you'd be surprised how quickly they get used to it."

"I guess someone's going to get even more spoiled," I told Moobie, who slunk back inside her pet carrier. She purred as I petted her. Even though the news had been worse than I had expected—the cancer, the need for surgery, the heart murmur, the collar—I still felt as if a burden had been lifted from my shoulders and placed on Dr. Hedley's alongside the marmoset, python, toucan, and other zoo critters.

MANY, MANY, MANY years ago, after discovering that Grand Rapids–area businesses weren't fighting tooth and nail to harness the power of my newly acquired Master of Arts degree in English, I went on unemployment—moving to Lansing for a change in scenery. The job market wasn't any better there. Or so I assumed without going to the bother of trying to find employment. I was too depressed. To fill the time, I slept in late, turned in early, and padded my afternoons with serial naps. At my lethargic peak I was probably in bed upwards of fifteen hours per day. Looking back, I couldn't help but feel regretful. I'd had the time, the opportunity, and the mental wherewithal to sleep a full twenty-four hours a day, yet I hadn't taken advantage of the situation.

I'd struggled to catch up on my sleep ever since, and that passion for just lying around and doing absolutely nothing, preferably in a state of unconsciousness, was a trait I shared with cats. And the visit to the vet had somehow exhausted me. But Moobie, the grand dame of the snooze, was apparently too joyful about being back home to sleep.

She sauntered up and down the headboard shelf heaped with books and magazines. Fortunately she knocked down no more than three issues of the *New Yorker*, two Perry Mason mysteries, and a hardcover reference book on mushrooms. It seemed petty to interrupt my nap just because these had fallen on my head. I was finally stirred to action when she poked her head behind the curtain, pulling it back wide enough to burn my eyelids with a dull winter glow. I clapped my hands to interrupt her. "There's nothing out there for you." Agreeing, she hopped back down onto the bed and initiated her usual routine of tapping my face fifty times with her paw before toppling into a heap at my side. She prepared to sleep and let me sleep. Or so it seemed.

The licking started just as I began to drift off. I thought I might be able to ignore a rhythmic lapping by pretending I was hearing the distant ocean, but her licking rose alarmingly in volume, approximating the sandpapery smack of a cow scouring her calf with a six-pound tongue. I inserted my hand beneath her chin to deflect her from her target, and she applied her ministrations to my palm as if it were an extension of her body. Then, in order to lick her hind foot, she sat up and leaned backward against my cheek.

I wanted to be angry with her—and for a flash I was. But

as I made the bed, she rubbed against my leg, purring, folding herself in half, and staring at me with a beatific attitude. My petulance evaporated. How flat and how dry my life would be without her. How I'd miss her easy companionship if her surgery turned out badly. Then she raced me to the bathroom and I daydreamed about moving to a cat-free village on a lush rain-forest mountaintop.

I FELT BETTER about my life with Moobie, Agnes, and Lucy after visiting Linda's friend Jo Ann, who had talked me into setting up her new answering machine so that it actually answered calls. As I was squinting at a folded slip of tissue paper that masqueraded as the user's manual, Jo Ann's tabby, Tommy, sauntered into the dining room. He immediately began rubbing against my leg, leading me to wonder if Moobie had e-mailed Tommy about the sucker who was visiting.

"See that popcorn?" Jo Ann pointed to kernels on the rug next to her TV-watching chair. "I have to make him popcorn every night, and if I don't, he'll come up on the chair and start doing this." She tapped my arm with her fingers. "If I ignore him, he moves up to my shoulder, then he jumps on the back of the chair and starts to whack my face. He packs a wallop."

Jo Ann earned further punishment if Tommy's food dish wasn't filled completely to the brim or if his water bowl was contaminated by the very same kibbles that he himself would carry and deposit there. "He insists on bacon in the morning," she said. "He sits at the table and eats it off a paper plate."

"He eats at the table?" Linda asked.

She made a weary face. "I have to do it. He makes me. And anytime I leave, when I come back he'll hide under the bed to show that he's mad. And if he smells my hand and I've been petting another animal . . ." She shook her head as if the consequences were too terrible to contemplate.

"Does Tommy take a nap with you?" I asked as we put on our coats.

"Every afternoon whether I want to or not. And I have to lay a certain way just so he'll be comfortable. Never mind if I'm comfortable or not."

It was clear that Jo Ann was even deeper under the claws of a cat than I was. It chilled me to think that I could share a similar fate. Only the fact that we didn't eat bacon at our house stood between me and the abyss.

LINDA AND I ushered in the morning of Moobie's surgery sitting on the edge of the bed drinking a cup of coffee. The bed had just been made and Moobie had already claimed Linda's pillow. Things already felt off: the songbird mug I usually drank from occupied the top rack of the dishwasher along with all my other preferred cups.

"What kind of idiot designed the pet carrier?" I asked. Nervous about the surgery, I prattled on to fill the silence. "You can't reach in to pull your cat out if the cat doesn't want to come out. Theoretically you could remove the whole top, but that means loosening six thumbscrews. You have to open the grate and turn the carrier on end to shake the cat out. I hope I don't have to do that with Moobie."

"What do our calendars say today?" Linda asked.

I groaned. We used to have a page-a-day Audubon bird calendar that brightened up our mornings, but the publisher stopped publishing it. To replace it, Linda bought an *Obscure Word and Phrase Origins Calendar* that was as dull as a Dutchman's breeches, then a *This Day in History Calendar,* which turned out to be uneventful. In disappointing succession came the *Ripley's Believe It or Not!* and the *Cartoons from the "New Yorker"* calendars. The task of plowing through all four burdened my mornings with a weight that not even my songbird mug could have lightened. The anvil was heaviest when we had failed to read the entries for several days in a row and Linda felt obligated to catch up.

As she grabbed the stack of calendars, I asked, "Didn't you get a new flower catalog? Heirloom roses or something?" We looked at that instead. I hoped to carry with me to Dr. Hedley's office a mental image of incandescent red Mr. Lincoln blossoms instead of a two-headed calf.

I said my good-byes to Moobie before dropping her off. Though I had boundless faith in Dr. Hedley, I knew that accidents could happen.

"Keep that heart going for me," I said. She rubbed her head against my hand as I reached into the carrier and tweaked one of her ears.

Months dropped off our page-a-day calendars and continents

drifted apart until Dr. Hedley phoned shortly after lunch with the news that the procedure had gone perfectly. "We can keep her overnight," he said. "But if you're anxious to have her back, you can pick her up after five. She'll still be a little rocky from the anesthesia."

"It's better for her to be home," I said. "She's not used to being away."

Since we had been bringing him all sorts of animals to treat over the years, Dr. Hedley assumed that a groggy cat wouldn't cause us worry—and it didn't. Panic was more like it once I had eased Moobie out of the carrier and tried setting her on her feet in the living room. When her front legs worked, her back legs didn't, and when her back legs worked, her front half drooped like a washcloth. She seemed intent on dragging herself hither and yon, and yonder lay a grumpier than usual Lucy who growled at her approach. We stowed her in the bathroom beneath the shadow of her beloved spigot, and she soon fell back to sleep.

She hadn't been saddled with her Elizabethan collar yet. Dr. Hedley had shown me how to slip it on and off, but recommended that we wait to see how she acted first. With any luck, she would leave the incision alone and could recuperate cone-free.

I had a brief respite from worry at dinner when Linda asked, "Do those smell okay to you?" as I was about to shovel green beans into my mouth.

"Why wouldn't they be okay?" I asked.

"I had two containers of leftover vegetables in the refrigerators, and I thought I gave the oldest ones to the hens, but now I'm not so sure."

"You need to start using a marking pen," I said. "You can write 'Hens' on the freshest leftovers and 'Husband' on the borderline stuff."

ANXIETY SHOOK ME awake at five thirty the next morning when I would have preferred a pair of paws thumping on the door. I flicked on the bathroom light. Moobie looked the same as she had the night before and didn't lift her head to purr when I stroked her back. Rushing to the kitchen, I brought her an irresistible pick-me-up of shredded tuna, hoping it would play the role of smelling salts and get her on her feet. But she barely opened her eyes as I fluttered the saucer under her nose.

After uncovering the birdcages and giving Bella the chance to amputate my ear while I diced up grapes, I made a second attempt to feed Moobie. She managed to stand up and stay up, but she turned away with a perfunctory sniff. Scooping up a dab on my finger, I followed her around the bathroom on hands and knees, keeping the tuna near her snout until I finally broke through her resistance and she licked my finger clean. I offered her a second dab, and moments later she attacked her plate.

Two hours later, Linda phoned me at work with the welcome news that Moobie was acting like her old self. "She's on my pillow again," she said. "But she isn't licking her leg. She might not even need that awful collar."

When I came home I found her snoozing on the couch, relaxed and untroubled by an impulse to molest her sore. It appeared that we had licked the tumor, and Moobie had licked licking it.

MOOBIE WASN'T THE only cat in the house to have apparently turned over a new leaf.

Lucy was trying, I thought. Apart from my nightly shampoo tête-à-têtes with Lucy, I hadn't succeeded in drawing her into any normal catlike activities with me. She preferred maintaining an attitude of injured aloofness. Immediately after stepping out of the shower, I tried rubbing one of her dusty mousie toys in my hair and batting it around on the rug. "What's that thing, honey?" I asked her. "Better get that nice-smelling mousie!" Ignoring the scented rodent, she lunged at my hand instead.

Our only activity was when I assisted her in exiting the house. Loosening her bulk from her wooden throne, she would hop down to the floor and scuttle up to me with surprising nimbleness. The tiny "mew" that issued from her cavernous mouth always gave me the briefest moment of confusion wondering if a newborn kitten had slipped into the house. Then she would pierce me with her imperial dowager stare and trot to the door, assuming that I followed on her heels. I was only too happy to serve on these occasions, and Lucy enjoyed glowering at a natural tableau from the front side-walk. Invigorated by the outdoors, she would meow loudly an hour later, insisting to be let back inside. And although she'd had the entire yard at her disposal — lovely gardens with fine black topsoil, ornamental bushes, earthy-smelling mulch — a visit to the royal litter box typically followed.

Linda had never wasted a second trying to coddle her like I did. So I was stricken with envy later that day when Linda told me about their shared moment. While she was brushing the bunnies prior to putting them to bed, Lucy had scurried under the dining room table with a look of expectation taking the place of what Linda described as "her usual under-taker expression." Responding to the onus placed on every cat owner to read a cat's mind, Linda realized that Lucy wanted to be brushed.

On the floor in front of the rabbit cages, Linda leaned over Lucy, brushing her carefully. "She licked my hand in appre-ciation," Linda said. "I was touched at first. But when I didn't brush her just the way she wanted me to, she gave my hand a little nip."

The next evening, I sneaked into the dining room to catch Lucy actually enjoying something. Flopping over on her side, she took a perfunctory bite at the brush but stretched her rear legs in an appreciative manner. To keep the fangs at bay, Linda praised Lucy as she brushed. "Don't you look smooth and well-groomed," she cooed. "You're going to look pretty for the kitty calendar. Yes, you're going to lead the kitty parade. You'll look beautiful when you pull the cart full of mice."

In my presence, Linda's flattery seemed to embarrass Lucy. She flashed me the accusatory look of a secret drinker caught in the act. She cut the grooming session short by raising her substantial bulk off the floor and barging past me.

"I guess I spoiled it for her," I said.

"It wasn't that. She wasn't too sure about pulling the cart full of mice."

The mental image of Lucy in a kitty parade put me in such a good mood that even though I was overdue for my recurring dream about getting stalked by leopards, I had an undisturbed night's sleep. Still cheery at breakfast, I chattered on about my childhood fear of encountering a garbage truck as I walked to kindergarten. "I think the noise scared me," I told Linda. Before leaving for work, I bent down to scratch Moobie's head.

"Oh no," Linda said. Moobie had created a new sore every bit as red as the first red spot.

We wrestled with Moobie on top of the bathroom vanity to attach the Elizabethan collar. I laid down a towel in front of the sink thinking that the process would go more smoothly if we kept her from sliding across the countertop. But her churning feet launched the towel through the doorway. Clutching the gyrating cat, I tried saving Linda's liquid-soap dispenser from a similar fate, but a kick sent it thudding to the floor. Despite her gaunt skin-and-bones frame, Moobie shrugged me off with impressive strength. "I can't hold onto her," I said. As I countered a series of seismic shocks that shot my toothbrush up my sleeve, Linda succeeded in slipping the cone over Moobie's head and tying the drawstrings into a bow.

"Got it!" she cried.

As soon as I relaxed my grip, Moobie jerked her head and flung the collar against the wall and into the bathtub. Linda retrieved it as I dove forward and clamped the cat's scrawny shoulders in the crook of my arm, and I somehow installed the collar again as Linda subdued her hindquarters. Despite the pinioning, Moobie stuck my stomach with her rear claws and then neatly stripped off the cone with her front paws. A referee materialized in the doorway to ring the bell that announced the start of round three. Summoning upper body strength honed by decades of cleaning houses, Linda held Moobie still this time while I replaced and cinched the cone. When we had finished, my hair was stuck to my forehead, my shirt was in disarray, and I had forgotten what a good mood felt like.

I set Moobie down in the front hallway, and she quickly proceeded to beat the cone against the wall. I was shocked by how huge and clumsy it was. The translucent white collar completely hid her head unless you were looking at her from the front, and I couldn't even begin to imagine what it must feel like to wear the thing. I carried her to the middle of the floor where she could oscillate and agitate in comparative safety, and she began to walk in circles. Regaining her equilibrium, she broke into a run, but the bottom lip of the cone caught in the carpet and nearly flipped her over.

By trial and error, and with our guiding nudges, she eventually bumped her way into the closet for a nap. I sat with her for a while, telling her what a good, good girl she was. Then I shuffled off to work wearing an invisible cone of unease.

I STUMBLED OVER simple tasks all morning as I worried about Moobie blundering through the house. Back home, I trotted into the dining room to find out why Bella was squawking and was alarmed by the lamp that had fallen underneath the table. But we didn't have a lamp with a white shade and none that were decked out in fur and feet. Moobie had gotten her collar stuck inside the rungs of a chair that she normally would have scampered through.

I freed her from the chair, and she made a beeline toward the living room. Her head bounced up and down as she walked. The cone dipped to scrape the linoleum, her neck lifted it up, and then the weight of the cone forced it earthward again in a series of movements reminiscent of a windup toy. The mechanical cat never made it through the doorway. The rim of the cone snagged on the metal strip separating the dining room floor from the faux-tile pattern in the hall. Still, she bulldozed forward until I picked her up and set her down on a square of sunlight on our bed.

Later, as I headed upstairs to my office, she braved the

climb to join me. But her Elizabethan collar turned each step
into a wall. By trial and error she managed to flop her funnel
onto the stair above her and follow with her front feet, only
to wind up with the opening of the cone pressed flat against
the front of the next stair. Her face was plunged into darkness until it occurred to her to back off slightly and shake her
head. A glimpse of the stair above her began the process all
over again. It was a painful thing to watch. I held myself back
from interfering, deciding that she had to learn to do things
for herself. Then almost immediately I relented. She could
learn while I was at work when I didn't have to witness her
suffering.

Even on flat, unobstructed flooring, she had a tough time
navigating the house. Lacking peripheral vision, she turned
too late and collided with walls instead of angling around cor-
ners in a slinky feline manner. The cone played havoc with
her acoustical perceptions, too. At the rattle of a doorknob
behind her, her ears would pivot backward but fail to home
in on the noise. She would look from right to left ahead of
her instead. I approximated the effect by cupping my hands
in back of my ears; the whoosh of air through a furnace duct
all at once grew higher pitched and jumped close to my head,
skewing my sense of three-dimensional reckoning. Considering how much a cat relied on hearing, it had to drive her
crazy.

Despite all this, even from a room away she didn't have any
trouble recognizing the soft plop of a spoonful of canned cat

food hitting her bowl. Eating was a problem, though. The lip of her collar bumped against the rim of the bowl, keeping her more than a tongue's length away from the goodies. Drinking per her usual fashion was out, since I knew her funneled face wouldn't fit beneath the bathroom spigot. And it wore me out watching her get ready to take a nap. Sleeping meant trying out a dozen positions until one finally struck her as less uncomfortable than the others, until the collar was neither too stretched nor compacted on her neck.

We helped her out as much as possible, carrying her to her destination when we figured out where she was going, lifting her cone off the carpet when she tried to plow a furrow through it, and, of course, holding her food and water dishes—a task which always seemed to fall upon me.

Although she didn't have to wear the cone twenty-four hours a day, I couldn't see removing it. Just a few abrasive licks would negate hours of conification, and it seemed cruel to replace the collar once she had enjoyed its absence. It was better that she simply get used to the cone until we could toss it away once and for all.

I BECAME DISTRACTED from my fixation on Moobie when a snowstorm with banshee winds knocked out our electricity. For three days we depended on a sputtering generator for light, heat, water, and toast, and we had to be careful which appliances we ran at the same time, or the generator would cough and threaten to shrug off its mortal ignition coil.

The power finally flickered back on, and that was when I noticed a dramatic change in our collared cat. Although the cone still bobbled as she marched across the living room, it no longer dipped down far enough to snag the carpet. And it barely oscillated at all as she trotted up to the so-called entertainment center, where her jar of kitty treats resided.

She had also conquered the stairs. True, she still lurched from step to step in drunken rabbit fashion, flopping her head around like a jack-in-the-box. But when she made it to the top and parked herself next to my office chair in hopes of dispossessing me, I noted a mixture of triumph and entitlement in her that I had never seen before.

She continued to pretend that she couldn't eat from her bowl unless I held it for her. But later I caught her in the hallway doing her wok-lid impression. She had completely encircled her bowl with the cone and then plunged her face into the food—immersing her in a perfect world devoid of sights and sounds as she crunched away on kibble. But as soon as she raised her head and saw me, she banged her cone against the wall as if I were witnessing the tail end of a terrible accident. She meowed urgently, requesting me to hold her dish.

Moobie hadn't merely adapted to her collar. She had turned it into an advantage over the coneless beings around her. Lucy and Agnes were intimidated by the catlike being with the weird headgear and gave way whenever she approached, which led to a proportionate increase in boldness on her part. She invaded their territory, taking over a choice sleeping spot on the arm of the couch or sashaying up to me demanding to be the center of attention while I was petting one of them. And while she feigned helplessness at her own dish, she blatantly wielded her cone as a shield while she crunched and slurped their food.

A few days later we were awakened by a sharp rapping at the bedroom door. "What in heaven's name is that?" Linda asked as we sat up in bed. My first thought was that someone had broken into the house—either a burglar or a woodpecker. Then we heard it again and identified the source. Instead of raking the door with her paws to rouse us, Moobie was using the lip of the cone to bang against the wood. Linda sleepily let her in, and she bounded up onto the mattress toward my pillow, planting her feet on my chest and thrusting her face into mine.

Linda snapped on the light. Inches away from my head, a bright white kitty face swam against a white plastic background, a feline sun burning brightly in a terrible cosmic void—the countenance of a fussy cat goddess commanding tribute from her human subjects. I threw off the covers, shrinking back, fearful that I would tumble, body and soul, into a maw of bottomless desire.

"She actually likes it," I told Linda with a shiver as we sat on the edge of the bed sipping coffee a few minutes later. I clutched my beloved songbird mug in my hand, but it gave me little comfort as Moobie shot laser-sharp begging looks at me. I had already given her food once and water twice. She was probably holding out for bacon.

"She knows that as long as she's wearing it, she's going to be spoiled."

Howard the dove hooted and cooed from the dining room. The parrots traded morning vocalizations, with Bella struggling to whistle *The Andy Griffith Show* theme song and Dusty asking, "What does the duck say?" Theirs was a relaxed and innocent world that suddenly seemed far, far away.

"It isn't an Elizabethan collar. Not to her." I held my palm in front of Moobie's face to try to thwart her stare, but she moved two steps, sat down again, and continued to pummel me with her high beams. "It's her funnel of happiness," I said.

CHAPTER 6

· ·

The Cats of Winter

Putting the cone on Moobie proved to be a whole lot easier than getting it off her. Quite as unexpectedly as fall turning into winter, moths munching on a favorite sweater, or Lucy finding new ways to overshoot her litter box, she showed poor judgment as her incision healed. We had tried removing her funnel three times since her surgery, but she kept licking the former site of the dreaded red spot and turning the spot red again. So the funnel kept going back on.

As I sat on the couch leafing through a field guide to birds, she hopped up beside me and banged her cone across the pages. Rewarding her with the attention that she craved, I picked her up, set her down on the floor across the room, trudged back to the couch, and continued reading. Moments later she reclaimed her spot and with a few bobs of her head slapped the book out of my hands. I reached into the cone to scratch her ears. Then for the third, fourth, fifth, or sixtieth time that day, I parted the fur on her leg and examined the faint pink hyphen of fully healed flesh where the red spot had once shone brightly. The site had never looked better.

"There's nothing there but a scar this time," I told Linda as she breezed by with her binoculars. Sick of the house, she was about to brave the cold and slog down to the river, looking for birds along the way. Back before we were married and long before I ever cared about any animal, she had piqued my interest in birds by pointing out a rose-breasted grosbeak at her cabin up north. I'd been infected with the birding bug, but it took more than the usual nuthatches and chickadees to convince me to abandon the comfort of the house.

"You don't want to come?" she asked.

"Don't slip on the ice," I said.

As she pulled the bread bags over her socks, I motioned to her to take a peek at Moobie's leg. "There isn't even the slightest trace of a sore now. I'm going to take the collar off and she can lick all she wants. She can't hurt anything."

Once again I proved to be as accurate as a place-mat horoscope. By lunchtime she had transformed a patch of glowingly healthy pink skin into an unhappy crimson blotch, forcing me to put the collar back on her again.

"Why would you do that?" I asked the giant kitty head, which tried to hypnotize me into shaking out fish-flavored treats. "Absolutely not," I informed her.

"She's ruined the fur there," Linda said as I rubbed my hands together to remove the oily treat crumbs from my palms. "She'll have to wear that cone until the fur grows back. As long as the area feels weird to her, she'll bother it."

"And us."

SHORTLY AFTER I had refunneled Moobie, the phone rang and I heard my friend Bill Holm's voice on the answering machine. "I thought I'd dispense cat wisdom, but either you're out or you saw my name on the caller ID." I drew a blank at first. Then I remembered. Three or four days ago—an eternity in terms of my limited memory—I had left a message on his machine asking for his advice on the deconing procedure.

Bill either knew more about cats than any other person I had ever met, or he had deluded me as thoroughly as he deluded himself. Right or wrong, he spoke about all things cat with an air of incontrovertible authority, and he insisted that cats were smarter than people. I still hadn't decided if this was his way of elevating cats or denigrating people. Probably both.

After we had dispensed with the usual unpleasantries, I recapped my problems weaning Moobie from her collar. "Could she be licking her shoulder because she wants to keep wearing the cone?"

"Cats are convoluted beings, but it's usually pretty easy to tell what they want—and she wants to lick herself," he said.

"So what should I do about the collar?"

"Get one for yourself."

"Get what for myself?"

"If the collar makes Moobie happy, it might lift your spirits all the way up to morose. And you might even get Linda to spoon-feed you." After a few more minutes of enumerating the benefits of a cone, Bill returned to Moobie. "Put a dab of bottom-shelf liquor on the spot. Try Smirnoff's. She'll hate the smell, she'll hate the taste, and she'll leave her leg alone."

"Does that actually work? Have you tried it?"

"Have I tried Smirnoff's? It didn't keep me from licking my shoulder."

"Did you try it on your cats?"

"I've got better things to pour it on than Zoey or Zippy. But there is a liquid that you can buy to keep your cat from licking itself. I think it's got 'sour' in the name. But it isn't 'whiskey sour' or I'd know about it."

I SHOULD HAVE done the smart thing and called Dr. Hedley for advice. But I was embarrassed to tell him that three months after Moobie's surgery we still hadn't completed the defunnelification process. Instead I decided to consult with my sister Joan, who had owned cats for decades.

At Joan and Jack's house, I peered out onto the porch and spotted three cats that I had never seen before. "You can look at them, but you can't go out there," she said. "Jack can. He practically lives there. And they're getting better with me."

I was shocked at the notion of having cats that couldn't be visited without a special kitty visa. But until the new arrivals had passed a feline leukemia test, they couldn't join house cats Linus, Winston, Libby-Lou, Finnegan, Max, and Gizmo. "We don't know how we're going to get them to the vet," Joan said. "They're feral and have never been touched by anyone. The mother cat would shred me if I tried."

Joan and Jack lived in the city. A quarter of a mile from their house was an abandoned boxcar where the neighborhood strays hung out. A gray adult had been lurking in their backyard teaching two kittens to decimate the local bird population. Jack started feeding the cats and letting them sleep in the garage. But it was getting below zero at night, so he decided to catch them.

The gray-and-white youngster that Jack had named Milo lay on his back under the kitty climber flailing his feet at his caramel-and-white sibling, Carmelita. Ember, a calico adult, watched them from the top.

"I started camping out in the kitchen and checking the live trap every hour on a wireless video camera I bought," Jack told me.

"You watched them on a video camera?" Linda asked.

"I was afraid that if a cat got caught in the trap overnight, it would freeze to death, because it can't move around enough inside the trap to stay warm. I caught little Milo right away, and he started crying when I put him on the porch. The gray adult and Carmelita bolted and wouldn't go near the garage again. So I bought a second trap, put one in the backyard and one in the driveway, and spent a week on the couch getting up every hour. Finally I caught both of them at the same time in the backyard trap."

I stared harder at the scene on the porch. "I don't see a gray adult cat."

"Funny thing," Jack said. "I ended up catching Carmelita and this cat I'd never seen before. But Milo stopped crying and ran right up to her, so I knew she was his mom, the one we named Ember. I'm trying to get them used to being around people. I bought one of those cheap DVD players, and I sit out there with them watching movies."

"So you bought a wireless video camera, two live traps, and a DVD player for the sake of three cats that you can't even touch," I said.

"And a kitty climber," Joan chimed in. "Don't forget their kitty climber."

"And I was about to ask your advice," I said. When I explained Moobie's problem, Joan told me that Bill had been on the right track after all. "You need a spray called bitter apple," she said. "It tastes so bad they don't want to lick the spot. The only time it doesn't work is if they lick off the bad taste and then keep on licking."

As we plowed back home through snowy streets, I couldn't help gloating a little about Joan and Jack. "I'm not criticizing their good intentions," I said to Linda, "but why would you take in even a single cat that was so wild you could hardly get near it?"

I ADMIRED JACK'S ability to formulate a plan and act on it. I'd spent a lifetime stuck in formulation mode. Linda was the initiator of activity in our house and rarely met a problem that she couldn't solve by assigning it to me. But in spite of hourly reminders from her, two days after visiting Joan I still hadn't gotten around to getting the bitter apple spray. Getting it meant having to go somewhere and talk to someone, which violated my ethics of inertia. Guilt would eventually spur me to act, but in the meantime I redeemed myself by rolling off the couch when Linda said, "Agnes wants to go out and I'm busy with Moobie."

I followed Agnes down the basement steps. Typically she would dash outdoors, linger a scant moment in the winter wasteland, and then beg to come back inside to score a treat from me. Both of us could follow the routine in our sleep. But this time when I threw open the door, the air was so cold that it blasted her into immobility. "Go if you're going," I told her when she refused to budge. I retreated shivering to a tiny circle of warmth that clung to the furnace.

She took exactly one step through the doorway. As soon as the dainty little pads on the bottom of her paw hit the ice, she zipped back inside. But instead of heading for her dish to await the spoonful of canned cat food, she raced up the stairs and ducked under the dining room table. Threading herself through a thicket of dining room chair and table legs and past the bird cages, she planted herself in front of the side door. She was certain that the miserable climate outside the basement door was the fault of a collusion between the basement door and me. If only I weren't so wicked, I would open the door in the dining room and admit her to a dazzling sunlit yard of warm, lush grass brimming with bite-size chipmunks.

Agnes refused to budge until I waved a hand in front of her face and attempted to back her out of the room. Aggrieved by my unfairness, she bleated underneath the table. I could simply show her the cold hard facts by opening the door, of course, but that meant subjecting Dusty to a gust of frozen air. I kneeled next to the parrot's cage, tracking his movements out of the corner of my eye, and then I lunged for Agnes—and missed. I straightened up and cracked my head on the table, and as I leaned back to whine about it, Dusty struck at me through the bars with a loud metallic ping that pitched me forward into the table and quieted the chatter of the dining room birds.

"Sorry," he told me in a perfect imitation of my voice. Agnes still hadn't moved.

On top of Dusty's cage lay a folded sheet that prevented him from nipping off the toes of any pet dove or parakeet foolish enough to make a landing pad out of his house during their out-of-cage hours. Shaking open the sheet, I tossed it over his cage as a windbreak and cracked the door just wide enough to prove that winter was winter no matter which portal you entered winter through. Agnes thrust her body past me, but the snow-covered steps displeased her. She fixed me with a glare so vile when she trotted back inside that I was glad she couldn't speak.

She sprang onto the back of the couch and turned herself into a sour donut—requiring no further services from me.

THE SUBJECT OF the bitter apple came up again as I was in the vulnerable state of pulling on my pajama bottoms. "You're going to the pet supply store tomorrow, aren't you?" Linda asked.

After I had adjusted the socks that I always wore to bed, I assured her that I would. "And definitely later in the week if something comes up tomorrow," I said.

Not long after she had snapped off the headboard lamp and changed from her regular cotton-polyester nightgown into flannel and then back again, switched the space heater on and off, given a nail a few blind swipes with an emery board, and generally flopped around like a halibut on a pier, a horrendous cat scream rent the night. This wasn't your typical offended-kitty outburst but a piercing shriek of pain that went on and on as I fumbled for my footing, shouting, "Turn on the light!"

I followed the wail to the bathroom to find Moobie twisted and hanging from the vanity drawer pull by her front leg. It looked very bad. But after I had rotated her forty-five degrees, lifted her straight up and out, and set her down on the floor, she gave her frame a brisk shake and started to amble away. She meowed indignantly when I snatched her up again and demanded that she let me know she was okay as I ran my fingers up and down the bone. Nothing seemed broken, but surely she must have sprained or dislocated the leg. I put her on the floor to watch how she walked, and she led me to the alleged entertainment center. She sat down on the rug and laser-beamed a stare that said, *Now that we're here, how about a couple of those kitty treats?*

"You're out of your mind," I informed her.

Back in the bathroom, I explained to Linda what must have happened while I washed the treat crumbs off my hands. Despite her coned condition, Moobie must have decided to try to drink from the spigot. By the glow of a bubbling snowman-head nightlight, she had made the leap up to the countertop without a hitch, but the loop of a faux-brass pull protruding from a slightly open drawer had trapped her in the process of hopping down. "We're lucky we were here when this happened," I said.

"We have to do something about her."

I threaded a hand towel through the drawer pull. "There."

"We have to get that collar off her. You have to get that bitter apple tomorrow."

"I will."

"And I didn't like you shouting at me about the light."

Unnerved by Moobie's close brush and annoyed at the unfair rebuke of my behavior under duress, I retreated to the upstairs bedroom to rummage around for something to read. Agnes complained when I elbowed her off the bed. "Go tell it to your mother," I said.

WHEN I HAULED myself out of bed the next morning, I checked on Moobie. She didn't show any ill effects from her brief stint as an extension to the drawer hardware. After feeding the cats, I plodded out to the mailbox for the Sunday paper, which got immediately added to the pile destined for the birdcages. I had given up trying to get through the newspaper faster than the parrots, and unlike me they paid equal attention to the advertising supplements and editorial sections.

The outside air didn't sear my bare flesh upon contact, which was an improvement over the previous day, and one lump of clouds seemed marginally less gray than the rest, hinting at the presence of a functioning sun. We had a chance of popping into double digits for the day.

"That cat's out there again," Linda hollered from the dining room.

A couple of weeks earlier, she had first reported seeing a white-and-black stray in the woods across from the trailer park. Staying in the shadows so as not to spook the cat, I peered through the bathroom window to find her sitting on the back deck close to the basement door. I suspected that she sought the heat that gushed out of our energy-inefficient house. "She must live in a hollow log out in the woods to stay warm," Linda said. She apparently read my mind about the temperature, though I couldn't claim credit for the cartoon log.

Forgetting yesterday's blistering cold, Agnes led me down the basement stairs and whined to go outside, but I didn't let her go. In a rare exercise of good judgment, I decided that it wouldn't be wise to mix a street-smart outdoor kitty that survived by outwitting small defenseless creatures with an indoor kitty that survived by outwitting a tall, skinny defenseless creature.

"Sorry," I told her. She complained with a whiny trill when I left her standing at the door. She recovered her sense of fun in time to try to kill me on the flight upstairs, tangling herself underfoot with the agility of a mountain stream. I wasn't necessarily afraid of an outright attack on Aggie by the stray. She didn't strike me as any kind of tiger as I peeked out at her through the bathroom mini-blinds again. But my visit with Joan had reminded me of the dangers of feline leukemia, and I wanted to keep Agnes safe for future attempts upon my life.

On Monday I motored to The Pet Supplies Megastore That Runs Out of Everything on my way home from work and nearly collapsed at finding a plastic bottle of bitter apple spray on a shelf. I waved off the cashier when she asked if I would like to sign up for The Pet Supplies Megastore That Runs Out of Everything Rewards Card, suspecting that my buying preferences would be shared with the Aisle Blockers so that they could more effectively obstruct my shopping.

Back home, as I stood in the living room holding the bottle in my hand, I decided that spraying it on Moobie constituted an activity and, as such, needed to be postponed. I stalled by pretending to read the label. "Don't apply to an open sore," I told Linda.

"Is that what it says?"

"No, it's just common sense. I'll give it a try after I take a nap."

Impeding my departure to slumberland, Agnes had curled up on my pillow nursing a bad mood. "You wouldn't go out anyway," I said. "It's really cold. And you might get chased by a ferocious feral kitty." She uncoiled as I stroked her forehead with a finger, turned into a wriggling eel as I petted her back, then surprised us both by biting my hand. I froze, wondering if I was so far gone that I had somehow mistaken Lucy for Agnes. She cringed as if I was going to whack her, something we hadn't seen since her earliest, insecurity-wracked days with us; we figured that a former owner must have abused her.

"It's okay," I told her. "You're just having a bad winter. You'll be able to go out again soon." She bleated like an unhappy sheep as she galloped away. I called Moobie, begging her to join me in the exquisite experience of an afternoon snooze, but she was already fast asleep on the couch. I slid under the pile of covers and surrendered to the heat and sweet unconsciousness. Twenty minutes later I sputtered awake to the tap,

tap, tapping of Moobie hitting the bedroom door with her cone. I opened it, and she sauntered in with her funnel bobbing like a pigeon's head.

I scrunched her against me on the mattress and located the tiny little nothing that remained of her incision scar. Her leg would never be more fully healed than now. I sprayed the spot with three pumps from the bitter apple bottle. Curious how bitter the bitter apple might be—apple with a trace of bitter, or mostly bitter with a hint of apple, and why add any apple at all?—I touched the nozzle with a fingertip, applied the residue to my tongue, and felt my face cave in on itself. It made alum seem sweet in comparison.

"That'll fix your wagon." I untied the cone and slipped it off her head.

My heart sank as she gave the spot a lick, paused to curl her upper lip in displeasure, then settled in for a serious tonguing session. Apparently she was doomed to wear the collar for the remainder of her life. She hopped down to the floor and I followed. Foregoing the usual wait for service at the bathroom spigot, she trotted up to the nearest water bowl and drained it dry, which floored me. I couldn't remember the last time I had seen her drink from a bowl. Returning to the couch, she resumed her snooze.

Later in the week I considered returning the spray for a refund, since the bottle was still full minus a mere three puffs. But I didn't want to give the cashier a fresh opportunity to suggest that I sign up for a rewards card.

Even though I've never liked to initiate activity, I set a whole lot of wheels in motion when I opened the door and let the white-and-black kitty onto the porch. Petting her as she munched kibbles, I consoled myself with the thought that I hadn't actually been the decision maker. I was simply the hand that opened the door, and she had done the rest. But I still had to live with the consequences.

The last thing that we needed was another cat. Three cats were as demanding as all of the ducks, geese, and parrots combined, plus they refused to repeat snappy phrases like Dusty. A fourth cat would also shatter the complex social arrangement that Agnes, Moobie, and Lucy had worked out. Agnes hated Lucy and Moobie. Lucy disliked Moobie and Agnes. And Moobie ignored Agnes and Lucy. With her combination of nervousness and blazing independence, the stray could only add what Linda called "trouble with a capital *T*." I worried about her through the night.

As I swung my legs out from under the covers the next morning, I prepared myself for two possible scenarios. Now that the rain had stopped and the world had frozen again, the cat would have the left the premises and returned to her beloved fields of ice. Or I would step into a tableau straight out of a kitty calendar with the stray snoozing happily on her pillow. Instead I found myself in the middle of a merry-go-round. Not just the stray, but the stray and two other cats revolved in a perpetual motion machine of on-porch, off-porch pursuit and retreat. I couldn't imagine how long this had been going on, but if the activity could be harnessed it had the potential of solving the energy crisis.

I was still groggily attempting to process the idea of three cats on our porch (though seldom all three at the same time)—and I hadn't even needed Jack's high-tech video trapping gear to put them there—when Linda came in. "Saddleback!" she cried. "And who's the other one?" According to Linda, the cat that she had named Saddleback for his distinctive fur pattern had been making appearances in our yard for the past several months in pursuit of Agnes. The second lothario was a strapping male tabby that we had never seen before. He paused momentarily, threatening to gum up the Tyrolean clockwork, lamenting loudly that any female would reject him.

As our white-and-black stray slipped outdoors to the porch steps, the tabby hurried behind her with Saddleback in tow. She planted her toenails in the frozen ground, poised to race away across the yard, but zipped back onto the porch instead and hopped up onto her cardboard box. From the ramparts of the carton she defended her femininity, hissing at the tabby and then Saddleback when they padded back inside to flank her. Darting between them, she raced down the porch steps and halfway to the mailbox, spinning the wheel of kitty activity another full revolution.

Then she arrowed back inside. I continued my imitation of a useless plank as Linda shot out her foot to dislodge the gallon jug of water that had been propping open the front door.

It slammed in the faces of the males, who suddenly noticed our presence and remembered that as outdoor cats they were duty bound to shun us. They didn't stick around long enough for me to pass along detailed directions to my sister's house, but I pointed in her general direction as they trotted off.

"Don't tell her I sent you," I called after them.

THIRTEEN YEARS AGO on a frigid New Year's Day, Agnes appeared in our backyard scavenging sunflower seeds that had fallen from our feeder. She didn't zoom off when she saw my face. She all but leaped into my arms and commanded me to bring her indoors. Once inside she clung to my lap like a burr, conspicuously ignored our pet birds, and immediately mastered the litter box. It was clear that she wasn't a feral cat. She was someone's pet who had been dumped on our doorstep.

And when I first met Bill Holm, he was sharing an apartment with a small, ferocious cat named Abby. As we listened to Harry Nilsson's *Aerial Pandemonium Ballet* on Bill's appallingly bad record player, Abby emerged from beneath the sofa to sink her toenails into my ankle or her teeth into Bill's dangling hand. A few days later, as Bill was watching *The Joker's Wild* on his unspeakably terrible black-and-white TV, she jumped up and clawed his eye, sending him to the emergency room with a scratched cornea. It was clear that she wasn't a house pet. She was a feral cat who had been dumped on him by a friend.

Our stray was neither house cat nor feral cat. She was somewhere between the two, as I learned when I tried approaching her later that morning. "You'd better stay in here," I said to Linda at the living room threshold, probably echoing my brother-in-law's words minutes before he bought a DVD player for his porch. "She seems to trust me, but she doesn't know you yet," I added, ignoring that Linda had been the cat's original object of affection.

I extended a hand to the stray as I stepped onto the porch. Although she didn't try to claw a tunnel through the wall as a feral cat might have done, she vaulted up onto the farthest windowsill and eyed me warily. An overloaded coatrack, an unused exercise bike in front of it, Linda's boulder collection, and a space heater in front of that kept my glad-handing at arm's length. I ducked out the front door and around the side of the porch to the window, huffing in the cold as I greeted her with my mildest, "Hi, honey." The sill turned catless. I realized that I was no more appealing than Saddleback.

I tried another tactic and dropped a handful of kibbles in her bowl. She made a beeline for my ankle, raised her heart-shaped face to mine, and delayed attacking the food until I leaned down to pet her. When she had finished eating, she squeaked, clearly requesting that I replace the water jug. And as soon as I propped the door open, she skittered outside, raced around the corner of the house, and disappeared. I reached the dining room window just in time to watch a gray

smudge rocketing down our neighbor's driveway and wink-
ing out as it approached the riverbank.

I should have been pleased; I didn't want to live like Joan
and Jack. Instead, I felt let down.

"That's the last we'll see of her," I said.

With each visit to the window my longing for her grew. Few
cuckoo clocks could equal my vigilance. Yet just before evening I stepped out to replenish Lucy's kibbles and there was
Frannie curled up on top of her cardboard box. *Frannie.* The
name just then had popped into my head and suited her perfectly, pending spousal approval. Though I had wanted her to
return with all of my heart, now that she was here my heart
muttered second thoughts. But I had named her and that meant
she belonged to us—if she was capable of belonging to anyone.

The next afternoon Linda called from the basement
and told me to come see the unusual ducks on the river. I
threw on my coat, slung my binoculars around my neck, and
Agnes trotted out the basement door behind me.

The gloriousness of the day startled me. Bright blue sky
pressed down on the bare trees, dislodging tufts of snow
and squeezing drops from icicles. "See them?" asked Linda. I
couldn't figure out what she meant. We were still a good three
hundred feet from the Grand River, shrouded by branches,
shrubs, and fog gathering on my eyeglasses until I unwound
the scarf from my nose. "Those flashes of light," she said.

Following the blur of her waggling finger I picked out a few pulsating specks on the ribbon of water.

"I don't see how those could be ducks." I hurried anyway, looping my arm through hers and cracking ice beneath our feet as we scurried down the driveway. Agnes arched her body in pursuit of us. Scouring the snowy ground, she ran directly for us then veered off in an arc of disinterest that purported to put her in our vicinity by happenstance.

As we drew past the neighbor's house, Agnes abandoned her pretended fascination with a buried jar lid as an excuse to gallop toward us again, this time rubbing against my boot as she fell in at my side. "See them?" Linda asked. I nodded, hanging back behind the willows. The sun glinted off the white sides of five ducks in the unfrozen center of the river as if from polished metal. Some of the ducks faced the current, some bobbled backward while I peered through my binoculars. "Buffleheads!" I called out—black-headed ducks with a cone-shaped white patch on the head—a new bird species for our woods and a welcome alternative to Moobie's funnel. Hearing their name, the ducks pulled a Rumpelstiltskin, suddenly flying off.

Linda hadn't gotten a decent look. I had spoiled the moment by trying to get too close. But she was happy that I was happy, and Agnes was even happier as she lingered and raced, lingered and raced, following us back home to the basement door. The only thing that pleased her more than being outdoors was being outdoors and showing off for us.

Spring was still a dim light in the distance, but it had inched close enough to cause winter to momentarily relent. Agnes breathed in the coming change of season and liked what she smelled outdoors.

Inside was a different matter. Her good mood petered out after she trotted up into the living room and pressed her nose into the crack beneath the door to the porch. She caught the scent of the new cat and growled in trepidation.

"I know just how you feel," I said.

....

CHAPTER 7

The Cat You Can't Do Anything With

Frannie was only with us for forty-eight hours before Linda and I had our first disagreement about her. It began with a shriek from the kitchen as a mouse launched itself at Linda from the cupboard under the sink. I made the mistake of laughing and as a result was immediately assigned an activity.

"We need to get the live trap fixed," Linda said.

I fished it out of a drawer. "An elephant stomped on it." I waggled the metal door flap, which would only open about a quarter of an inch. "But if scallops invade, we're ready for them."

The stomper wasn't amused. "Then we need to get a new one. I'll call Bonnie at the hardware store and have her hold one at the front counter." Clearly I couldn't be trusted to find a trap on my own.

I tried to improve my standing by coming up with something better. Pointing at Frannie on the porch, I said, "There's our solution."

"You mean our problem," Linda said.

"You've seen her outdoors. She's a lean, mean killing machine."

"And we're not letting her in the room with our birds."

"No, not right away," I said, though she was looking domesticated to me already. "We can teach her how to act."

"Frannie?" Linda said. "A can't isn't like a dog. You can only teach a cat to do what it already wants to do, and some are worse than others." Illustrating the point, Lucy plopped down to the floor and strode toward the litter box. Linda watched her like a hawk. I turned away.

I had ever-increasing faith that Frannie would turn into a lap cat. But after just two days, she had become a porch barnacle, which was the last thing that I would have expected. I figured that she would use her carton as a field office for launching raids upon the squirrels. But she clung to the pillow on her box through high and low tide alike, detaching herself mainly to crunch kibbles from her bowl. Just when I started worrying that she and Lucy had somehow traded bodies, I realized that Saddleback and the heartbroken tabby had been staking out our house. I saw the pair lurking behind our monster pine, and after dark the tabby sidled onto the outside steps to serenade Frannie.

Still, Frannie wouldn't allow me to remove the water jug,

pacing anxiously once the door banged shut. She wanted the security of a ready exit. So when the tabby stepped over the water jug I lectured him on proper decorum. My macho presence struck fear into his soul for a full twelve minutes, but when he strolled back inside, Linda's single hand clap drove him out the door for all eternity. He must have discussed his banishment with Saddleback, because after that hand clap, we were never to see them again.

With their departure, Frannie began exploring her new space and found it confining. But she wanted in instead of out. She jumped up onto the picture window between the porch and living room and marched back and forth along the sill while I was trying to follow the narrative intricacies of *Hogan's Heroes*.

"That cat's knocking down my pictures," said Linda, referring to her blue jay greeting cards that flew off the sill like real birds whenever anyone breezed by.

As Colonel Klink and General Burkhalter discussed the superiority of the German Gonculator compared to the American model, Frannie raked the porch door with her claws. But instead of shooting into the house when I eased the door open, she hurtled over to her box and eyed me with suspicion. "You can't come in with the other cats until we get you tested," I explained. "But you can go outdoors if you want."

I sank slowly to my knees in front of Frannie with a Gatling gun round of pops issuing from my joints and embarked upon a soothing monologue on the subject of disease detection and treatment. I wasn't just concerned about the possibility of feline leukemia. A discolored strip ran down Frannie's nose and mouth, and a vet needed to determine if it was caused by illness, injury, or something else.

"We don't want our new honey to be sick," I said, leaning over to plant a reassuring hand on her back. As my fingertips brushed her fur, she swatted me away. It was a clawless correction, but just barely. Her flattened ears told me that I had better back off. I retreated to the living room. "Klink, you idiot!" General Burkhalter shouted.

With Frannie only allowing my touch as a side dish to a meal, I wondered how I'd ever be able to pick her up and plunk her inside a pet carrier. I didn't want to traumatize an already nervous cat. And I shared my sister's fear of getting shredded. I considered calling Bill for advice but changed my mind. No way was I going to waste my time with him.

BILL'S LINE WAS busy, so I phoned Joan and asked her if she had managed to get her strays to the vet. Things had gone smoothly with the two young cats, she said. Jack had set a cat carrier on the floor with a towel inside, and Milo decided that popping in and out of it and scrunching up the towel was just about the most fun a cat could have. Jack snapped the carrier door shut while he was busy playing. But Carmelita was warier than her brother and didn't see the charm in a plastic box.

"I had no choice, Bob," Joan told me. "Jack held a carrier

with the opening pointed up at the ceiling. Then I grabbed Carmelita by the scruff of the neck. I'd never touched her before, and I just grabbed her." She guided Carmelita's dangling back legs into the open mouth of the carrier, latched the grate, and expressed a few expletives of relief as Jack spirited the pair outside to the Trooper.

The siblings were tested, Carmelita spayed, and Milo neutered. Then they spent the weekend at the clinic. The plan was for Jack to take the mama, Ember, in on Monday when he picked up the kittens, but Ember had a little scheme of her own. On Sunday morning when Joan went out to the porch to check on her, Ember was giving birth to an orange-and-white kitty. Two more babies followed.

"We don't need more cats," she told me, but I had stopped listening. Instead I was wondering whether a drugstore pregnancy test might possibly work with a cat. I was superstitious enough to halfway believe that my life had begun to mirror Joan's. She ended up with three strays on her porch, I ended up with one. Her female cat had given birth to three kittens, so Frannie would give birth to one—or six, or nine, or twelve. Suddenly it seemed more imperative than ever to have Dr. Ziaman examine her.

That night I carried a saucer with canned cat food out to the porch. To make the entrée especially bewitching I had warmed it in the microwave, though Frannie was still so thrilled by the concept of food without fur that she would have fallen on the treat even if it had been frozen solid. While she was busy scarfing down the chow, I examined the floor around her carton—no partially knitted booties, no book of baby names. Still, I had to be sure. As she licked the plate, I petted her, then I slid my hand down to squeeze her abdomen. I didn't know exactly what I was expecting to find, but once I had my fingers under her belly I thought I'd see if she would let me pick her up. But she broke free with a whine.

I replenished her dish with a second helping, but she wouldn't give me a second chance. The encounter had eased my mind, however. She had felt way too scrawny to be on the brink of motherhood even with a litter of equally skinny kittens, and she didn't shred me during my attempt to pick her up. Those were the positives. On the negative side—the side of the street that I lived on—I fretted that the dark streak on her face might be as troublesome as Moobie's dreaded red spot.

Frannie reprised her windowsill pacing performance that night while we watched the pig Arnold Ziffel inheriting millions of dollars on an episode of *Green Acres*. "I'm calling Dr. Ziaman tomorrow morning," Linda said.

I OFTEN HAD trouble sleeping the first few nights after a new animal had arrived. I would awaken from a sound sleep to thrash around for hours gripped by the "Oh no, what have we done?" syndrome. I experienced one of my worst bouts when we had taken in a parrot named Stanley Sue. This was years before an easily accessible Internet existed for finding out everything about anything. I read all the books and magazine articles about African greys that I could find, and Linda phoned a few area bird owners, but I still felt woefully unprepared to deal with the complex creature who made sobbing sounds in her sleep during her first weeks with us. The same feeling of unreadiness came back to me again with Frannie.

It seemed as if I was hardwired to her anxiety. When she scratched on the door and we couldn't let her in, I worried. If she ducked outside to harass the local wildlife, I worried about that, too. I worried whether she would get along with our other cats. I even worried when I saw her peacefully curled up on the pillow due to worry inertia.

A few hours before her vet appointment, I went down to the basement to root through our pyramid of pet carriers for the one that would best fit Frannie. Naturally it lay beneath a couple of goose-size transports. As I wiggled it free from the stack, I was startled by a snarling commotion overhead. Agnes' trademark banshee shriek clashed with a scream the likes of which hadn't been heard in our house since Linda made pickled radishes.

Linda and I reached the scene of the fight at the same time, but we weren't able to break it up. We didn't have to, because a closed door stood between the pair of quarreling cats. Agnes must have gotten fed up with Frannie scratching to come in and tried attacking her through a matchstick-thin crack underneath the door.

After I shooed Agnes away I popped the door open to find a ruffled Frannie holding her ground. She hopped up onto the windowsill and scanned the living room for Agnes. I had no way of knowing it at the time, but the Battle Behind the Door was the Fort Sumter event of what historians would later refer to as the War Between the Cats. We were witnessing the definitive first battle.

I HAD HOPED to take a calm cat to the vet. If I wanted to do that, I'd have to take Lucy instead of Frannie, who whined piteously and clung to her pillow as I tried to pick her up. She cried all the way to the clinic, and though she didn't match Moobie in volume, her mouselike squeaks stabbed an ice pick into my heart.

I had made an appointment with Dr. Ziaman, but she had been called away on an emergency, so her partner at the clinic, Dr. Post, took her place. It was the first time I had met her, so I wasn't prepared for her deadpan manner. I wasn't too surprised when Frannie nestled against my hand when the vet strode into the room, since I represented the lesser of two evils. I was shocked, though, when she let Dr. Post flip her over like a pancake.

"I'm looking for any evidence that she's already been spayed. It isn't an operation that a cat needs to have twice," she said. Frannie barely moved as Dr. Post checked her ears for parasites. "We're going to have to hire you to teach good behavior to the other kitties."

"It's not like her to be cooperative," I said. "You must have a special way with cats."

"You'll have to tell that to the one that bit me this morning." She spread her fingers to show me the tooth mark on her hand.

A blood test brought the good news that Frannie was negative for feline leukemia, but the streak on her face wasn't easy to diagnose. I have a pair of scars on my upper lip as a result of a bite from a friend's husky, so I wanted to suggest to Dr. Post that our mutual marked lips indicated that Frannie and I had shared numerous incarnations dating all the way back to Atlantis.

"It could be a deep infection," Dr. Post said. "Or we might be dealing with a food allergy. We'll treat it as an infection first and see if it clears up."

She sent me home with an oral antibiotic and the unhappy prospect of having to hold Frannie and squirt it down her throat twice a day. I held out a faint hope that a cooperative Frannie might emerge from the carrier instead of a skittish, stubborn cat, but she immediately sought the protection of her cardboard box.

FRANNIE HADN'T BEEN giving us more trouble than we could handle yet, but Linda had a solution. A woman at the store up the street had mentioned that she needed to get rid of her chickens and had decided to give them to a neighbor who would turn them into roasters. Befriending a woman at a busy supermarket who wanted to dispose of her poultry could only happen to Linda. It gave me yet another excellent reason to use the automated checkout lanes.

"Please scan your first item and place it in the bag," the computerized voice might urge me, but never, "Please pick up the first hen and place it in your car."

I didn't feel too put-upon adding what Linda's new friend Janet had described as a few hens to our flock, but due to a long-standing grievance against alarm clocks, mechanical or biological, I balked at taking her rooster. And the notion of acquiring another large aggressive bird gave me pause, since Linda's parrot Dusty enjoyed stalking my stocking feet. I knew roosters that were capable of worse.

"Teddy doesn't bother anyone," Janet told Linda, and the fact that the barn was far out of earshot during my morning, afternoon, and nighttime sleeping hours helped Teddy's case. So we agreed to visit Janet and round up her purportedly small flock.

The opportunity to grab hens provided me with a welcome break from my now twice-daily ritual of grabbing Frannie. I'd clutch the struggling cat to my chest, and Linda would pry open her jaws and dose her with medicine. But Frannie never got used to the procedure; even after three days, when I picked her up she squeaked in shock as if nothing like this had ever happened to her before. Fortunately her selective memory meant that she returned to her normal pet-me-while-I'm-eating self right away.

Janet's cramped henhouse was about as roomy as the interior of Linda's Ford Escort. This seemed to argue for a minimal number of hens, but she pulled one bird after another out of there, like clowns from a circus car. I stuck my head inside and observed that she had divided their quarters into compartments that essentially turned a coop for egg layers into an egg carton for hens. "Their quarters were supposed to be a whole lot bigger," she said. "The Bosnians who built it read my plans wrong and converted my inches to centimeters."

"Let's put Frannie in the house and move the chickens to the porch," I said. "They'll think they're in the Taj Mahal."

"It would be a whole lot more peaceful than having Frannie there," Linda said. It was a logical assumption, because our own chickens had never caused us any trouble. We didn't expect that these would be any different, though they did look rather strange.

"What's wrong with their feathers?" I asked Janet as I slid the carrier containing Teddy into Linda's hatchback.

"They've picked at each other a little bit. The missing feathers will grow back."

I hoped that they didn't try to pick at me. That was Frannie's job.

WE IMAGINED JANET'S sardine-can chicken flock luxuriating in the spaciousness of our barn. But once we released them, they huddled in a corner behind the stairs, arranging themselves in a chicken coop–size rectangle. When I slogged outside after dinner to dole out treats, the rectangle of hens expanded slightly as the first handful of bread pieces and kale hit the floor. I tossed some greens in front of my feet.

Victor commandeered the food, greedily gobbling it up and launching his bulk at any duck or chicken that dared to intrude upon his bounty. The hens advanced when I distributed treats toward the center of the floor, except for Teddy, who seemed to lack the hunter-gatherer skills of the females.

"The new hens are still nervous," I told Linda back at the house. "I hope they get over their shyness."

I needn't have worried. The next night, the shrinking violets hung back in the shadows as I flung food in their direction. But as I lobbed a few chunks of bread toward Victor, six of the balding hens swept in from the gloom and vacuumed up the crusts right under his beak. Victor's bullying tactics proved too slow for the hyperactive, tattered chickens. Then, egged on by Teddy's rallying crow, the hens launched one lightning-fast foray after another, swooping in wherever a crumb of food hit the floor. I switched to scattering treats in the widest possible arc, hoping that the hens couldn't be in all places at once. In the midst of their feeding frenzy, Teddy launched himself at me with spurs outstretched. Pawing the straw with his feet like an enraged bull, he started to come at me again—until I bopped him in the head with a plastic pitcher.

"How were they?" Linda asked as I returned to the house.

"They've formed a gang," I said. "It's *Night of Living Dead* out there. I was lucky to get back in one piece."

"Well, they'd better shape up, or they'll find somewhere else to live."

"Take them back to the supermarket. You saved your sales slip, didn't you?"

THAT SATURDAY WAS THE night that we would let Frannie into the house, and I was nervous. "Don't expect miracles," Linda said as she put the plates on the table.

For the umpteenth time, I repeated the story of how cooperative Frannie had been with Dr. Post and how this was a sign of good things to come. "And I'm sure she's been in a house before," I said as Linda passed a bowl of pasta salad. "Or she wouldn't be begging to get in. I'm sure she'll do okay."

Actually, I had grave doubts about the ability of a rambunctious cat to slot into a house where nothing much ever happened. But I figured that the sheer dullness of our lives would numb her into placidity. The process might take time, but we would make it work, I decided. Linda seemed to be thinking similar thoughts as she stared at nothing and chewed. "What do you think?" I said.

"I'm glad I made my own pasta salad instead of buying it at the store," she said. "They use one of the cream-based sauces that can kill you."

After assuring myself that no lethal sauces lay in ambush on my plate, I opened the door for Frannie.

As Frannie made her entrance, Moobie greeted her with a perfunctory hiss that simply indicated, *Hello, I'm here.* Lucy treated her as she treated Moobie and Agnes, somewhat diffidently, yet whacking her with a front paw as she strayed

too close to the monarch's throne and then challenging her
when Frannie attempted to usurp the royal feed bowl. Agnes, however, took umbrage at Frannie's very existence. She
maintained a low growl when Frannie entered the room, the
undertone rising and falling depending on Frannie's proximity. After a while, when she had had enough, Agnes launched
herself at Frannie with a fearful scream before retreating to
another room.

Frannie hid behind the entertainment center while we
watched TV, pacing back and forth in the narrow slot amid
the spaghetti of power cords and cables between the cabinet
and the wall. "There goes our picture again," I said as she
jiggled loose a crucial wire during the episode of *Mission: Impossible* in which the Impossible Missions Force convinced a
mobster played by William Shatner that he'd traveled back in
time thirty years. I felt thirty years older after I had managed
to reattach the disconnected cable and she promptly yanked
it out again. Exhausting her role as TV critic, she darted back
onto the porch, only to rake her claws against the door as
soon as I closed it.

In the days that followed, Frannie had no use for me apart
from wanting to be petted while she ate. In her case it wasn't
due to a case of great big fat cat sullenness. She simply had
an aversion to people. When an affectionate mood managed
to penetrate her, she would press herself tenderly against a
door frame, chair leg, table leg, or any leg but mine. When
I praised her beauty and intelligence, she would roll over on

her side and elongate herself on the rug, urging me to pet her. But if I tried, she would shoot up and run off as if she had just seen my dreadful face through the bathroom window.

"I don't think she likes me," I told Linda.

"She's crazy about you," she said. "She just isn't the cat you thought she'd be."

I had hoped for a nap-time companion in the Moobie mold, a cat that would be undyingly grateful for having been rescued. But Frannie was apparently ambivalent about the whole darn thing.

In a couple of weeks she had trained me to regard her as a delicate glass ornament to be admired from a distance and seldom handled. Mine was the heart of glass when I had to cart her off to the vet for spaying. But just as Dr. Post had told me, spaying was an operation that no cat needed to have more than once. Surgery had revealed that Frannie didn't require a hysterectomy after all because she no longer had a hyster to ectomize.

I brought home an unhappy and bedraggled white-and-black kitty from the vet. Based on how long it had taken other cats of ours to recover from spaying, I had expected her to remain stretched out on her pillow with her nose buried in a magazine while eating bonbons for a couple of days. But once she had shaken free of the anesthesia by the next morning, she began petitioning to go outdoors.

"You are supposed to stay quiet," I told her. "You got cut

open. You've got stitches." So intent was she on escaping to the yard that she rubbed her face against my ankle, bolting only when I leaned down to pet her. "Nope," I said in response to her whine.

If she wasn't under, on top of, or behind a piece of furniture seeking shelter from the storm of human activity—a mere trickle in my case—she stationed herself in front of some closed door desperate to go through it.

She intended to make sure I understood that all doors led to the one and only door that she actually wanted open. To keep me from ignoring this desire, she would choose a moment when I was reading to hop up on the headboard and threaten to knock Linda's angel figurines into the unreachable purgatory place behind the bed. A glance in her direction would slingshot her to the front door and activate the begging mechanism.

AT LEAST FRANNIE was phobic rather than aggressive, unlike the zombie hens who had decided to pick on our small female Muscovy duck, Juanita. Less than half the size of a typical barnyard white Pekin duck, Juanita dwarfed the bigger birds in her enthusiasm for treats. Should any of them waddle between her and the scrap of kale she coveted, she had only to stretch her neck in a gesture of menace to send the interloper scuttling off.

This was how the classic pecking order worked in our barn. Personality as much as physical strength determined a bird's ranking within the flock, but the zombie chickens wouldn't follow the rules. Devoid of either grace or cuteness, they punished Juanita for cornering the market on both. They launched themselves at her in gangs of four or five, driving her from the food and then continuing to harass her with claws outstretched in harpy mode. One morning, when Linda opened up the barn, she found the little duck huddled beneath an ancient wardrobe.

"I don't know what made me finally think of Sjana," Linda said when I straggled home from work. "The Lord must have put her in my mind. I'd never really talked to her before except once when I called to ask her if she took in baby birds." Sjana, a wildlife rehabber who lived nearby, agreed to help Linda box up the zombie hens. Wielding a trout net, Linda scooped up the chickens and stuffed them in pet carriers, while Sjana braved the fowl with her bare hands.

"Who caught Teddy?" I asked, picturing prolific bloodletting.

"There was nothing to it. I swished him in the net and put him in one of the carriers."

Linda's friend Carol had agreed to take the chickens. She was used to dealing with large beasts with cloven hooves, so the zombie hens wouldn't bother her a whit.

Thanks to my Catholic school upbringing, I tended to see the hand of invisible forces stirring the pot of the most commonplace soup. Thus I associated the arrival of the zombie hens with our run of bad luck with Frannie. Linda's removal of the hens had exorcised the evil. Suddenly, instead of begging to go out, Frannie seemed to have lost the urge to dash out into the snow. She started acting calmer, spending whole minutes in the middle of the living room. And she was looking better, too. The antibiotics had gradually triumphed, and the dark streak on her muzzle was fading, though she only let me examine it from a distance. I was looking for my binoculars in hopes of getting a closer view when Carol phoned Linda.

"You'll never guess where your chickens spent the night," she said. "They flew over the fence and roosted in the garage. We had to round them up and put them back into their pen."

"Maybe they were homesick and they're working their way back to our place," Linda said.

"Don't even think that," I said. Considering how much trouble Frannie had caused us, I felt as if the chickens had already come home to roost. Now I was waiting for the bluebird of happiness.

AND IT DID seem as if Frannie was changing her restless ways. But as another bout of bad weather hit, she raced out onto the porch whining to go out. She raised and lowered one hind leg, spun around, then raised and lowered the other leg. I had never witnessed this odd pistonic activity before and it unnerved me. "You can't be that desperate," I said, and she cried more shrilly in response. "It's nasty out there. You won't like it." I cracked open the door to let a blast of cold air hit her face. "See." I opened it a little more, demonstrating that she had my permission to make the sensible decision to stay inside. Moving so slowly that I never doubted she would choose warmth and comfort over icy air and a hard snow-pack, she glided past me and out.

I followed as if I had intended on taking a stately stroll, anyway, and merely wanted a word with her, but she didn't let me get close enough to make a grab. She darted around to the back of the house, concealing herself under the pine for a while, then she switched to her old spot beside the pump house. At least, I thought, she was sticking close to the house.

But by dinnertime she had completely disappeared. I called and called and called for her, pushing through the wiry re-mains of last year's weeds as I scrabbled on top of a thick glazing of snow all the way to the river, around to the barn, and back. I drove up and down the street a mile in each direc-tion hoping that I wouldn't find a white-and-black body on the shoulder. I shouted for her some more from the driveway. Linda and I hollered into the darkness at bedtime, but we only succeeded in frightening a deer.

I tossed, turned, and gyrated all night, worried about her and fearful that she was gone for good. The next morning, I trundled down to the basement cloaked in pajamas and a desolate mood. I opened the door to call for her, but before her name reached my throat she materialized in front of me with a wild look in her eye that stopped me in my tracks. The look wasn't guilty or apologetic. It wasn't haughty or trium-phant, either. And it definitely wasn't the look of a pampered house cat. I stared at her, trying to make out what was there. Metallic yellow eyes like a snake's opening into some unknowable self stared back at me.

Those eyes said, *Here I am. This is me. This is how I am. Now let me inside.*

CHAPTER 8

....

The War Between the Cats

Having made her point about independence, and also having realized that a cardboard box makes a comfier bed than a patch of ice, Frannie stayed indoors during the final weeks of winter. And what icky weeks they were.

One early morning after a particularly hearty snowfall, I was pulling the covers off our birdcages when something crashed into the window. I zipped outdoors with a flashlight and discovered a screech owl huddled in our spruce tree. This had happened once before. Holes here and there in the snow suggested an explanation. Instead of skittering around in the open with bull's-eyes on their backs, the local mice were safely making their rounds via tunnels in the snow. With rodents off the menu, the owl must have decided that a pet parakeet or dove would do.

The mice didn't like the winter weather any better than the owl. As the snow piled up over the next several days, the mice piled inside our house. I realized that the situation was worse than usual when Linda told me that she'd heard squeaks coming from the plant stand in the dining room.

"They must be coming from inside the walls," I said.

"No, they're coming from the plant stand."

I didn't hear a thing, and Linda's excavation of her pencil plant, Christmas cactus, aloe vera, and Moses-in-the-Bulrushes failed to uncover evidence of a hidden mouse civilization.

The next day she said, "I'm definitely hearing baby mice." She pressed her nose against our boom box that sat in front of Moses. "Pew. They've got a nest in there."

I refused to believe it until I turned the boom box around and sniffed a small round opening that supposedly enhanced bass response. One whiff of *eau de rodent* convinced me to retire the boom box to the barn.

"That cost me ninety-eight dollars," I said. "Now I need to buy a new one."

"You need to get a live trap, too."

As SPRING SPUTTERED in and the house mouse population continued to increase, Frannie began lobbying for a dash into the woods not only for the mud that she could track across our carpet but also to get away from Agnes. Instead of helping us with the vermin invasion, our black cat was doing everything she could to keep Frannie from settling in.

Agnes had never shown the slightest interest in the front porch. But suddenly, racing down the basement stairs to score a spoonful of Tastes-Like-Meat was passé. Now, the greatest epicurean delight resided in the bowl of kibbles in front of Frannie's box.

Agnes would wait until I let Frannie inside to spend time actively avoiding us. That was Agnes' cue to saunter out to the porch and loudly crunch on Frannie's food. She never chomped down more than two or three bites on any visit, boldly daring Frannie to do anything about it. When she tired of this, she would sit on the back of the couch and then fling herself at Frannie when The Little Kitty came out from behind the entertainment center. As a startled Frannie raced back to the porch, Agnes found herself scooped up in my arms and plunked down on the dark side of the closed basement door.

"Are you going to put up with that?" I asked Frannie. For the moment, the answer was yes.

Agnes wasn't the only porch invader under our roof. We had decided to clear the pet closet of nonpet items like a heap of dirty laundry dating back to the reign of the first George Bush and a window fan that neither Linda nor I had remembered buying. Moving these to the basement created space for Lucy's litter box, and finally we had an unobstructed path from the front door to the dining room.

Starting fresh with a brand new utility tub, I cut a U-shaped opening into the corner this time, instead of the front. The innovation was a success. Lucy walked in on the diagonal, and as she turned to assume her favorite toilet posture, the tub wall directly behind her was at an above-the-tail height. Accidents decreased, but unfortunately so did usage. She disliked the size, shape, diagonal entrance, and closeted location of the new box and switched over to Frannie's litter box instead.

This was the extent of Lucy's forays across the battle lines. She and Moobie were noncombatants in the developing war between Agnes and Frannie. As long as Moobie could steal 99 percent of my office chair upstairs and flatten herself against my calf at nap time, she was satisfied to pretend that Frannie didn't exist.

THE DAY THE war escalated didn't start out so differently from any other day.

"Oh, don't eat that," Linda cried as I shoveled the second forkful of French toast into my mouth. I paused midchew as she sprang up and scraped the contents of her plate into the trash can under the sink. "Doesn't that taste funny to you?"

"I thought it was just me." I figured that the unusual flavor was due to the just-woke-up patina on my tongue. "What did you make it with?"

"I used a loaf of the whole wheat bread from the basement."

"Not the duck bread!" Sjana had brought us two garbage

bags bulging with outdated hamburger buns, bagels, dinner rolls, and other bread scored from a convenience store seconds before they went to the Dumpster. I had crammed as much of it as possible into our basement refrigerator. For the rest, it was a race between our barnyard critters and the onset of mold for possession. I hadn't realized that I was part of the competition, too.

"Sorry about that," she said. "It didn't smell stale. I'll make you an egg."

"I don't have time. I'm already running late." A metallic clinking from beneath the sink told me that I would be running even later.

"Oh, no. Another mouse." She fished out the live trap behind the trash can and handed it to me. "Can you stop somewhere and let him go?"

"Wouldn't it be easier to just let him have some French toast?"

"That reminds me," Linda said. "I've got to make sure that I didn't put that bread back with the other bread for the ducks."

"Why not?"

"I can't feed them stale bread. It wouldn't be good for them."

I wondered how much spoiled food I ate over the course of a week without knowing it, while our ducks, geese, hens, rabbits, and parrots got the fresher stuff. I also wondered why our mouse population kept growing even though the weather was getting warmer and we had four cats in the house.

I RECEIVED A partial answer when we shook off the winter cobwebs and took an afternoon walk. There was a warm breeze under a cloudless sky. It was a big day for Agnes, since it gave her the opportunity to be an outdoor cat again, and a big day for me because I had survived the French toast. Our black cat trotted along at our heels as we headed toward the river, but Frannie seemed reluctant to follow too closely for fear of getting attacked. She accompanied us at a distance as far as the neighbor's driveway before plunking herself down and turning into a white-and-black lump on the gravel.

Our walk to the river didn't take very long, because the river had come forward to meet us. Rapid snowmelt and two days of heavy rain had turned the high ground at the riverbank into a chain of small islands. Ponds filled the low spots in our woods, and I could hear the slam of tiny suitcases as grumbling mice abandoned their holes and headed for our basement.

At the water's edge we found a juice bottle, a chunk of a plastic foam cooler, a grocery bag, and a pressure-treated post, all washed up by the river. I dragged the post behind me, somewhat envisioning it doing something somewhere in one of our pens somehow.

A muskrat motoring through the cloudy water dove when he saw us. "He's probably looking for the secret passageway," I told Linda.

"What secret passageway?"

"The one that the mice take into our basement. He heard about the free food."

"And the lazy cats."

Right on cue, Agnes bounded ahead of us to strike a pose, sharpening her nonexistent front claws on the trunk of a fallen tree. Frannie shot past her, kicking up fallen leaves as she joined us on the path. They trotted along together, Agnes slightly ahead of Frannie, planting false hopes in my mind that they might become friends after all.

"Those two sure look alike," said Linda. "I'll bet you a horse they're related." Sure enough, both cats had the same build and small, heart-shaped faces. "They're standoffish in the house but friendly outdoors, and both of them are tomboys. And they follow us on walks like little dogs." Their mincing gaits were so identical that as Frannie pulled up directly alongside Agnes, they reminded me of a pair of huskies harnessed to a sled.

I dropped the waterlogged post before we returned to our neighbor's driveway. I imagined making a weeklong project of dragging it back to our yard a few feet every day. I was about to remark to Linda how nicely the cats were behaving when Agnes darted snarling toward the upstart. But Frannie wasn't the shy cat that she played indoors. She answered the attack with a whack to the face of her possible great-great-great-maiden-aunt. Triumphantly Frannie bolted ahead of Agnes and waited for us with shining eyes alongside the barn. Agnes fell behind me. The two cats were wary as we straggled through the basement door. The great outdoors didn't seem quite big enough for both of them at once.

AND THE OUTDOORS was shrinking fast as our woods continued to flood. Deer and turkeys sloshed to the hill behind our fence to eat mountains of scratch feed, while mice began flowing into our hundred-year-old house through every crack and chink. When they couldn't find an opening, we could hear them making their own at night. Bedtime was their favorite time for a snack of peanut butter on an outdated bread crust. Linda had just put on her nightgown when the trap beneath the sink clinked shut with enough of a jolt that we could hear it three rooms away with the door closed. "Remind me why we can't leave them in the trap overnight," I asked as she threw on her coat.

"Because they die of thirst overnight. And that defeats the purpose of a live trap." Zipping up her boots, she asked rather forlornly, "What do you think the temperature is out there?"

"It can't be any colder than thirty-four." I plumped the pillow behind my head. "Boy, this bed feels warm!"

She grumbled all the way out to the car, and I thought I could still hear her muttering as she drove away. Chauffeuring a mouse to its new lot in life was a fairly recent innovation. It dated back to last fall when I had trapped a mouse with a telltale nick in his ear and walked him a quarter mile down the street to the McDonald's 2 SMILES AHEAD billboard, figuring this to be an insurmountable distance from our house. The next afternoon we caught the same mouse again.

I dozed off thinking about the balmy weather that would soon blow into the state, sweeping in scads of migratory birds

for me to misidentify. Next month, Bill Holm and I were
headed to Nayanquing Point to search for the yellow-headed
blackbird. Common as mice in some Midwestern states, they
were as scarce as cat-chasing-mice in Michigan except for a
small breeding colony on Saginaw Bay. I was itching to see
one. Just as a flock of the boldly colored birds landed on my
outstretched arms and began to lift me up off the grass, Linda
slammed the front door and I tumbled back to earth.

"Where did you put the mouse?" I asked as she thudded
back into bed.

"Up to the turnaround just before Cumberland."

I tried floating back to the yellow-headed blackbirds, when
a metallic *clink* nudged me out of my reverie. I knew that
Linda had heard it, too, because she had stopped thrashing
around.

"Oh, no," she moaned.

"You didn't reset the trap."

"I didn't mean to."

"I'll dump him in the yard, and you can catch him again
tomorrow."

But she had already grabbed her keys and put on her coat.

The next morning, we barely recognized our woods.
The individual puddles and ponds had held a meeting during the night and passed a motion to join together in a swiftly
moving current. The river was about three hundred feet closer
to our door than usual. The flooding itself wasn't unexpected.

Each spring the low part of our woods turned into an aquatic playground for mallards, wood ducks, and Canada geese. But every five years or so melting snow and buckets of rain convinced the river to leap its banks. While the rushing water remained down the hill and behind the fence, the diminution in territory intensified the War Between the Cats.

I was listening to the shrimpy speakers on my headboard shelf trying to learn four warbler songs that all sounded like "pleased, pleased, pleased, to meet-cha." But all I could hear was snarling as Agnes ambushed Frannie beneath the so-called coffee table. "Okay, you two. Time to spread out." I shooed Agnes down the basement stairs and out the back door. After giving her five minutes to lose herself in the weeds, I propped the porch door open with the water jug and watched Frannie scamper out.

With our acreage reduced by flooding to a mere decimal point, their quick collision was inevitable. Agnes' trademarked shriek blotted out the olive-sided flycatcher on my CD. I should have skipped ahead to the catbird.

"What's Agnes doing up there?" Linda asked, pointing out the window.

"She must be chasing a squirrel or something."

"She doesn't usually climb the pine tree. She doesn't have front claws." She directed my attention toward Frannie, who was skulking around at the base of the tree. "That's why."

"She's not afraid of Frannie," I said. "She'd chase Frannie up a tree. There must be another reason, but she does seem to be stuck." Spotting my face in the window, Agnes meowed, and I answered her summons.

Standing on my tippy-toes I could just barely touch the bottom of the pine bough under her feet. By cooing her name and acting elated over our chance meeting, I coaxed her down the branch, snagged her leg, and pulled her from her perch as she bleated miserably. As I plopped her down on the cement floor just inside the basement, she whirled around, hurled herself across the grass at Frannie, and chased her around the tree. When they reappeared, Agnes was the one who was being chased. She tore into the basement and didn't slow down until she had rocketed up two flights of steps to take refuge in the upstairs bedroom.

"That was very, very naughty," I told Frannie, who pranced in front of the pine and rubbed up against everything in sight.

THERE WERE DEFINITE pluses to having the river so close. A pair of hooded merganser ducks had taken up temporary residence. I enjoyed watching the male raise and lower his crest as I raised and lowered my spoon at breakfast. I also liked wading down my neighbor's driveway until the water tickled the tops of my boots and the current nearly knocked me over.

There were negatives, too. The last time the river had flooded like this, it had brought a mink to our barn to kill three of our hens. So I wasn't taking any chances. I herded our ducks and hens into a room of the barn that we had mink-proofed by reinforcing it with chicken wire. I left the lights burning all night, and I tuned a portable radio to a twenty-four hour talk station to suggest a human presence, though one of a low intelligence. "If you owe money on your credit card, then you shouldn't *have* a credit card," the talk show host insisted.

The first three nights, I expended a year's worth of arm waving and racing around to chase the hens and ducks into the mink-proof room. After that, they filed in as if they had slept there all their lives. Their enthusiasm nearly convinced me to join them in the straw. Then Linda made a discovery that gave me second and third thoughts about wandering between the house and the barn after dark.

"You won't believe what I saw," she said, huffing and puffing after having hurried back from an afternoon wade through the high ground. "Down by Don's house. I thought it was a crow's nest up in a tree. Then I looked at it through binoculars and saw this giant paw. I thought maybe a hawk or eagle had killed some animal and taken part of it up to its nest. Then I saw that what I thought were sticks was actually fur—and I was looking at a bear."

I shook my head. "It had to be a raccoon. Bears don't come this far south."

"I've never seen a raccoon that big."

"Show me." I was certain that she had misinterpreted the size of some much smaller and completely mundane object, like a squirrel's nest or a speck of dirt on her glasses.

"We shouldn't go back there with a bear."

"I need to see it," I insisted, marshalling the courage of a man who knew there was no bear. We slogged toward the river proper. The flooding had receded enough that we were able to pick our way to the west side of our neighbor's house by keeping to the high spots. Linda led me up onto a finger of land, which we walked along as far as the second knuckle. At first I thought that the lumpy mass in a tree was indeed a squirrel's nest. But when I raised my binoculars, I saw that huge paw. This was a disaster. The ducks and hens were safe in our porous yet solid barn, but our geese occupied a pen that a bear could tear open like a bag of pork rinds.

Later that day I ran into Sjana at the store up the street, and she assured me that black bears were mainly vegetarians, and that he'd probably be gone by the morning. "It's just some little honey bear that the river displaced, and he's on the move." Still I felt uneasy when I braved our bear-infested environs after dark to check on the ducks and hens. Knowing that *Ursus americanus* was prowling around below Ursa Major made the darkness seem especially threatening.

I remembered that two weeks earlier Linda had dreamed about glancing out the dining room window and seeing a bear in the backyard. She ran out to protect our geese as they cropped the grass, unconcerned. When the bear started toward Linda, she woke up. I had pooh-poohed her nightmare at the time, but now it proved that, even when sound asleep, Linda knew more than I did.

SPEAKING OF BAD DREAMS, Agnes must have thought she was having a recurring one. I was staring out the window at the unusual spectacle of three bluebirds on our hanging suet feeder when I noticed a familiar bouncing bough across the yard. A triumphant Frannie had treed Agnes again. This time I didn't need to extract her from the pine. She scrambled down on her own and, just before running into the basement, hesitated on the deck to haughtily lick her rump, indicating her low opinion of Frannie.

Inside the house, Agnes remained the undisputed alpha cat. She would conceal herself in the living room, revealing her hidey-hole with a drawn out growl whenever Frannie ambled in. The noise was irritating enough to the people who were trying to enjoy some creaky old sitcom. But worse was when a heretofore undetected Agnes exploded from concealment with a fusillade of snarls and shrieks that scared the male human of the house far more the female stray, causing him to drop his bowl of ice cream.

Still, I was optimistic. "It's like when we introduce a new duck to the barn," I told Linda as I raced Moobie to clean spumoni off the rug. "The top duck will bully the new one for a while, then the new duck finds his place in the pecking order, and they all get along just fine."

Linda gave me a "you must be dreaming" look. "Agnes doesn't want to get along. She wants Frannie out of here."

"It won't stay this way forever. Frannie will learn to fit in."

I was right about things changing but wrong about the

nature of the change. While Agnes had previously assumed a natural authority, she seemed to be waging a defensive battle as she undertook her guerrilla campaign. Her attitude toward Moobie and Lucy softened. She couldn't enlist them as allies, but she did the next best thing by crossing them off her enemies list. Thus, I witnessed the unprecedented sight of Agnes drinking from the hallway water bowl mere inches away from mortal foe Lucy, whose face was submerged in the food dish. When Lucy came up for air and glared at her, Agnes hissed, but the reaction was as perfunctory and meaningless as telling her to have a nice day.

Agnes may have mellowed, but the invading mice had suddenly become more assertive. Linda's habit of ejecting them out of the car window rather than shaking them out of the trap a good distance away had finally caught up with her.

"Well, that was nice," she said. "I was on my way to the bank, and when I stopped at the traffic light at Bowes Road, a mouse was looking at me through the windshield."

I tried to picture this, but couldn't. All I could come up with was a man-size mouse driving a pickup truck in the other lane. "How could a mouse stare at you through the windshield? Where was he?"

"He was sitting in that groove in back of the hood by the windshield wipers. He sat there staring at me through the glass while I waited at the light. He was very accusing in the way he looked at me. And before the light turned green, there was a second mouse on the right side—and he was staring in at me, too! I suppose they were trying to tell me that the engine was too hot."

I struggled to decide which was stranger—the event that my wife had just described or her interpretation of the event. Frannie glanced up at me with a glimmer of amusement. "I'm glad you're getting a new car," I said. "Maybe we can get rid of half of our mouse population when you sell your Escort." Then I caught Frannie's eye again. "Especially since certain individuals aren't doing anything to pay their rent."

AFTER NINE DAYS the river had finally gotten that whole flooding business out of its system. That was the first night that I hadn't locked the ducks and hens in the back of the barn and made them listen to talk radio shows about the benefits of investing in gold.

We were watching *The Beverly Hillbillies,* waiting for guest stars Lester Flatt and Earl Scruggs to perform their song "Pearl, Pearl, Pearl." Just as Lester picked up his guitar and commenced to pickin', Agnes cannonballed out from under the rocking chair at Frannie. But instead of fleeing back to her cardboard box on the porch, Frannie discovered a whole new second story of life when she charged Agnes and chased her upstairs.

Alas, Frannie's entry into this higher realm was brief. Agnes installed herself as the fighting duchess of the upstairs and in the days that followed successfully repelled further incursions. Gone was her truce with the other two cats, though her fanged threats had no impact on Moobie. Completely ignoring Agnes, Moobie trudged up the carpeted steps every morning and ensconced herself on my office chair.

I felt bad about the situation. Dark, dour Agnes only lit up when she was outdoors. I hated to see her deprived of fresh air except for sniffs through a window screen, and she couldn't harass a chipmunk now unless it hopped up onto my keyboard to send an e-mail. But she was much safer upstairs than she would ever be outdoors with a busy road in front of the house and a bear in back. I wouldn't have continued to let Frannie out if being cooped up didn't make her so despondent.

Outdoors, Frannie let her triumph over Agnes go to her head. One Friday afternoon, Linda's driver Gwen dropped her off from her twice-a-week visit to the chiropractor. As Linda was gathering up her pillows, purse, and backrest from Gwen's backseat, Frannie trotted up to the car that was idling in front of our mailbox and whacked the rear tire with her paw to show it who was boss.

A week later, my accountant, Mike, drove up in his thousand-foot-long motor home/mobile office, unwound a yellow extension cord that was as thick as a fire hose, and dimmed the lights of everyone on our power grid as he plugged it into our porch. Balanced in a doll-size swivel chair on the passenger's side, I recited figures to Mike for my belated tax return as he sat across the aisle in front of a PC, a laptop, a printer, a copier, an electric stapler, and several small appliances. "Well, now, there's a cat in here," he said blandly, peering at me over his half-glasses. I swiveled in time to see Frannie scamper down the aisle, exit, and streak across the lawn.

"Want a cat?" I asked as I shut the door to keep her out.

"No, thank you."

"Then you'd better check all the rooms in here before you leave."

Though the floodwaters had receded, our mice had pledged their loyalty to their home turf. When Linda started up her new car, a boxy Scion XB that we referred to as the bread truck, she was nearly blinded by a flare of "check engine" lights. "Maybe a slice of rye bread got stuck in the alternator," I suggested.

"Whatever's wrong, it's under warranty," she said—or so we assumed. The service manager informed me that an O_2 sensor devoured by mice wasn't covered and would cost us five hundred dollars to replace. Checking the Web, I discovered that damage to vehicles by rodents was a widespread problem and that the manufacturers of automotive electrical components apparently colluded with them. The O_2 sensors were being coated in a tasty soy-based material instead of plastic. After helping themselves to the scratch feed, sunflower seed, and duck pellets that abounded in our yard, the mice had enjoyed this exotic change of pace.

Either that, or they were getting their revenge against the person who had trapped them. I was glad that Linda had left the bear alone.

It seemed like any other Sunday morning when I opened the porch door for the winner of the War Between the Cats, held it and held it while she hesitated, and then watched her skitter down the front steps.

"How about you earn your keep for once?" I called. When she turned and looked back at me with flattened ears, I explained. "Keep the mice from our cars." My "check engine" light had come on shortly after Linda's, and I was starting to worry.

Normally I never let Frannie out until after lunch. But ecstatically singing birds, shockingly bright sunshine, and a silver mist across the grass made me want to bolt outside barefoot, and I was sure that Frannie felt the same way. Before she disappeared behind the monster pine, she slowed down and shot me another glance as if inviting me to follow. I felt an odd apprehension as Lucy oozed past me in the manner of a sluggish liquid rather than a surging force. I fought the urge to call Frannie back just because this wasn't the way we usually did things. It probably wouldn't have made any difference if I had kept her inside for another few hours—but for weeks I blamed myself for what happened next.

Lucy didn't venture the twenty feet out into the yard that it would have taken to guard the vehicles. She stuck close to the house, as if she were magnetically attached, rubbing up against the foundation while she rounded the corner and flopping down in Linda's iris bed for a nap. Even though she was no better at responding when we called her to come back in than Frannie was, we never had to search far for her.

She meowed at the side door around dinnertime, afraid of missing out on her evening teaspoonful of canned cat food. I had an especially greasy chunk of chicken dark meat for Frannie. She should have been able to smell it from the woods as I stepped out the back door with her treat plate in hand. "Chicken, Frannie," I said quietly, almost superfluously. Her pattern was to rocket up to the door, stopping only when she got within a foot of stepping inside and pretending to be gripped by indecision until I set down the plate. But I called and called and called, and she didn't show.

"She'd better not have run away," I told Linda as it started to get dark. My biggest concern about Frannie was that she would tire of mundane domestic life and hit the trail again.

"She'd better not think that she can stay out all night."

"She's been way too independent lately," I said. "She does anything she wants."

I marched down the neighbor's driveway, shouting her name with increasing anger that didn't exactly invite a response. From the riverbank, I heard the back door slam and Linda hollering for her. We met back inside without the cat, but as I sat down on the couch to grouse about that ungrateful Frannie, Linda went out again and came in quickly.

"I found her," she said. "She's lying out in the weeds in front of the barn. Something's wrong with her. She can't stand up, and she's got a big gash in her leg."

....

CHAPTER 9

Out of the Weeds

The pet owners in the waiting room at the emergency clinic had the stricken look of refugees. Their faces were pulled low with an expression of hopelessness that I hadn't seen since the last time I had gotten my driver's license renewed. A tube television tuned to CNN Headline News had been bolted to the wall to prevent us from slipping it into our pockets. It let us measure the length of our stay by the number of times we watched the story of a man in China who refused to move out of his apartment as a construction crew demolished the building around him. It was exactly how I felt as an injured Frannie lay motionless in a pet carrier next to me.

The check-in had proceeded smoothly. I explained how Linda had carried Frannie onto the porch, how she had cried and collapsed when we'd tried to stand her on her feet, and how she had been pretty much out of it ever since. After producing a credit card and the deed to our house, I was told that the emergency vet would see me right away. That meant I could expect to be here all night, I deduced from the pacing figures with cell phones in the parking lot.

To my surprise, within twenty minutes—which was a mere eye blink by waiting-room standards—a vet assistant whooshed through a swinging door and called Frannie's name.

My only previous experience with an emergency animal clinic had been abysmal. A loud, oafish DVM had handled our sick bunny roughly, which had led me to conclude that late-shift vets were the dregs of the profession who couldn't hack it during prime time. Dr. Fitzroy was bright, young, and inspired such calming confidence, that when she suggested Frannie needed an X-ray to make sure that her spinal cord wasn't damaged, I didn't immediately consider shuffling off and hanging myself. That could wait until later.

Back in the waiting room, I snapped open my phone and talked in hushed tones to Linda. I watched the Chinese apartment dweller defy the local authorities from his crumbling tower a few more times. The wearying boredom was therapeutic. It kept me from agonizing over Frannie.

Time slowed even more as Dr. Fitzroy clipped the first of two X-rays to a light box. I steeled myself for the worst, or would have, if I'd had any steel inside me. She pointed to a faint pair of streaks against white bone and said, "Her pelvis is fractured in two places."

"How serious is that?"

"It should heal on its own without a cast if you keep her still for a few weeks, but that isn't the only problem." She hung the second film next to the first and explained that Frannie's hind leg was dislocated. "Normally with a dislocated leg, we reposition it and pop it back into place. But we can't do that with Frannie without shattering the fractured pelvis."

"So what do we do? Will she have to have surgery?"

"You probably don't have to do anything. Cats' leg muscles are strong enough that they'll form a false joint over time. It's really amazing, but it works because their bodies are so light. It shouldn't present any issues, though she may limp a little."

"What do you think happened to cause this?" I asked and repeated the story of how Linda had found her in the weeds in front of the barn.

"There's no way to know," she said, jotting notes on Frannie's chart. "She could have fallen from a tree. From the gash on her leg, she might have been clipped by car. If that's what happened, she's probably lucky. Most cats that get hit by cars have much more serious external injuries." I could tell by her tone of voice that Frannie wasn't out of the weeds just yet. "We don't know if she has internal injuries. I see that her regular vet is Dr. Ziaman. Take her there in a couple of days for a follow-up. Let her rest until then and try to get her to eat."

She handed me a plastic bag stuffed with syringes so thin they resembled lollipop sticks. "This is for the pain. Give her one three times a day." Another bag of syringes materialized.

"She needs this antibiotic twice a day. Keep the wound on her leg clean."

I shuddered to think of once again having to give medication to Frannie, who disliked being handled under the best conditions. As I looked at her with concern, she fixed her eyes on mine and gave me the long, slow blink that a cat only gives to the people that it loves. She had never done anything like that before. That blink coursed through my optical nerves, pausing briefly at the tear ducts before setting my whole body aglow. If Dr. Fitzroy noticed my phosphorescence, she was too polite to mention it.

BACK HOME, WE pulled the lid off Frannie's cardboard carton and set it on the porch floor, positioned her favorite pillow on top of it, and gently slid her out of the pet carrier. She lay flat and exhausted, but sufficiently awake to swallow her meds when I tilted up her head. Outdoors a tree frog repeated a mournful note.

I went to bed with a strange sense of elation. Frannie's accident had swept aside everything comfortable in my tiny world. I worried that she had suffered internal injuries, and the knowledge that she was in pain clung to me like a ringing in my ears. But I still felt filled with light. The spark of love that had passed between us was a once-in-a-lifetime gift.

I woke up early hoping to find a greatly improved Frannie who was essentially her old self, though unable to walk. But she was nearly comatose. "She won't eat," I told Linda as I

teetered on the edge of our bed sipping coffee from an ORIGI-
NAL AMERICAN KAZOO COMPANY OF EDEN, NY coffee mug. Both
our *Dubious Daily Word* and *Ya Better Believe It!* calendars focused on medically grotesque subjects, so I set them aside.
"I tried chicken. I tried tuna from a brand new can. I even
heated up a dollop of Bits o' Liver and tempted her with it on
my fingers. She wouldn't touch a thing."

"You can't expect her to be hungry when she's in pain."
Linda said. That wasn't what I wanted to hear.

I would have welcomed some resistance when I daubed
the stitched-up gash in her leg with Betadine. And when I
pried her mouth open to dose her with her pharmaceutical,
she complained with an alarmingly weak rendition of her
usual squeak. These should have been two-person jobs, but
my vacant self proved sufficient. By evening she continued to
decline.

"I think we're going to lose her," I said. "There must be
some damage inside."

Showing my characteristic lack of good sense, I trudged
out to the porch before bedtime and blubbered my good-bye.
For once I could pet her as much as I wanted. When she lifted
her head to peer at me through cloudy eyes, I didn't know
whether she was acknowledging my messy farewell or asking
me to stop.

It seemed like a miserable irony that a cat who had survived on her own outdoors for months should perish in the
process of becoming domesticated. I could have locked her

inside and tried to ignore the pacing from door to door—and the flitting from window to window just to catch a whiff of the sweet world beyond our walls—but her unhappiness would have worn me down. I could at least have kept her in until after lunch, for all the difference that would have made. Fate had robbed her of years of chasing Agnes up a tree, turning up her nose at one canned cat food product after another, and evading my touch.

The next morning she had slipped so far into the bottomless pit of oblivion that it seemed cruel to force more meds down her. Linda made an appointment with Dr. Ziaman to see if anything could be done—including euthanizing her, if necessary. I took the morning off from work.

SHE PERKED UP a little by the time I hauled her carrier into Dr. Ziaman's office. With a cocked head she glanced around the room and yawned. This small activity was such a huge improvement over her previous comatose state she might as well have suddenly vaulted up to the ceiling. I wrote off her flicker of wakefulness to my having thumped her over potholed roads between our house and the clinic. Dr. Ziaman had another interpretation. "It's the painkiller," she told me. "It's too strong for her. You said you didn't give it to her this morning."

"They gave us the wrong painkiller?" I asked.

"It was proper for the day of the accident, but I think we should cut back now and switch to one that doesn't sedate her so much."

"So her painkiller is the problem?" I felt my elation surging again.

"We're not out of the woods yet." *Weeds*, I wanted to tell her. *Out of the weeds.* "I recommend we do a blood chemistry test to make sure that her internal organs are functioning correctly." She explained how elevated numbers in her blood profile would reveal a problem with her liver, kidneys, or something . . . but the explanation sailed right past me, because I was too busy mentally splashing around in a fountain of optimism.

"Normally we would take her into another room for the blood draw," Dr. Ziaman said, "but we don't want to jar her pelvis any more than we have to. So if it disturbs you to watch, you can look away while we take the blood sample right here."

I didn't understand what specifically might disturb me, but since I was easily disturbed, I stared at my shoes while Dr. Ziaman and an assistant went to work. "We usually draw blood from the inside rear leg, but we can't do that with Frannie. We have to lean her head and shoulders down off the edge of the countertop." I concentrated more intensely on my feet, but Frannie didn't utter a sound. "Dad, this is one brave cat," she said, making my day a second time not only with her praise of Frannie but also by addressing me in beatnik lingo. After running the test she explained that Frannie's major organs were, like, dreamsville, and that the scene should stay cool if she just hung loose.

Even though the big ticket items inside Frannie appeared to be undamaged, I was instructed to keep a close eye on her. "Make sure she eats, and also make sure that sometime in the next few days she uses her litter box. She'll hold out as long as she can, but she'll eventually use it if everything's all right."

"But she'll never get to it. She can barely move."

"Put some kitty litter in a shallow tray and move it close to her bed. Trust me, she'll use it when the time comes."

And if she needed a refresher course, I only had to open the porch door and Lucy would march out to show her how it was done.

I SHOULD HAVE felt great on the drive back home. But the further I traveled from the magnetic center of Dr. Ziaman's optimism, the glummer I grew. As my car clicked and popped to a stop in our gravel driveway, I had reverted to my usual negative self. I was always a bundle of nerves when one of our animals got sick, and Frannie's accident had turned me into one big throbbing synapse. When I delivered the good news to Linda that her injuries probably weren't life threatening, I managed to make it sound like a death sentence. The way I saw it, I still had a gravely injured cat and no reason to celebrate.

"We're in trouble if she doesn't use this," I told Linda as she prepared a new litter box for the cat. "She needs to eat—right now," I said as we surrounded her bed with bowls.

"She'll be fine. She just needs time to heal."

I shushed her when I heard Bill Holm's voice on the answering machine. I had completely forgotten about the overnight trip to Saginaw Bay that we were supposed to take. "He must be out of his mind," I said. "I can't leave when she's like this."

"Does he even know about her accident?"

Mumbling a non-answer, I picked up the phone. After getting the usual informalities out of the way, I told him what had happened to Frannie and explained that I was too worried about her to even think of taking a trip.

"Do you still have Moobie's funnel?"

My voice cracked in irritation. "What good would that do for a fractured pelvis, a dislocated leg, and possible internal injuries?"

"Not for Frannie. For you." Before I could complain about him wearing out a joke that I hadn't enjoyed the first time, he asked, "Remember how deathly ill Zippy was?"

"Yes," I lied, embarrassed that I'd been too absorbed in my own woes to recall that one of his cats had been sick.

"She was vomiting," he told me. "She stopped eating and drinking and looked like she was going to die. I was headed to work for a meeting, and I thought that by the time I got home, Zippy would be dead. She looked so pathetic and small and sad. So I knelt next to her in misery as she lay curled in a circle on a TV-room chair, and I said good-bye. But I also emphasized that if she wanted to get better, she had to eat. About three hours later when I came home, I opened the door, and she hopped off the chair and wobbled over to meet me. She made me follow her to her food where she took a few bites."

"She ate for you just like that?"

"And then she threw up in the dish."

"Oh, great."

"No, it helped. That was the moment she turned the corner, and now she's fine. Cats are such fighters."

I peered out the living room window at Frannie's flattened body on the porch. She lay on her side like a pork chop with a slight curve to her spine. I watched her abdomen move in and out as she breathed, which somewhat vaguely reassured me that she was still alive. "So I just need to tell her that she'll get better."

"Tell her you're going to Nayanquing to look for the yellow blackbird thing. She'll do the rest."

Jubilation briefly struck when I ducked through the doorway onto the porch and noticed that the minced chicken on Frannie's delft china saucer had vanished. I started to holler for Linda. But I stifled my excitement as I discovered a second empty plate, which had previously contained a dollop of tuna, and another plate formerly occupied by a lump of canned cat food. Over the two days since Dr. Ziaman had examined Frannie, we had placed these treats in front of her twice a day. Her untouched snacks were providing a bounty for Moobie, Agnes, and Lucy, who slurped up the hours-old but by no means French toast–quality outdated food.

A peek into the living room revealed the most likely culprit. Looking more self-satisfied than ever, Lucy avoided my eyes as she licked her chops. The level of kibbles in her bowl hadn't dropped a fraction of an inch since I had replenished it earlier that afternoon. "You couldn't wait your turn," I said. "Now we'll have to keep the porch door closed." Moobie changed direction when she saw me in the hallway and hurried into the bedroom—so multiple perpetrators might have colluded on the raid.

Armed with another round of meats, I did my best to convince Frannie to break her fast. "It's good!" I insisted when she turned her head away. A smudge of tuna on my finger earned a sniff, but no tongue.

"What are we going to do with you, honey?" Balanced on one knee, I scratched her neck and she surprised me by responding with a stretch.

Then I heard it. She actually started purring. I stroked her back, we exchanged slow blinks, and I floated back into the house on a wave of encouragement, and a short time later she proved me right. A chunk of chicken held no allure. She said *can't* to the canned food. But when I held a lowly bowl of kibbles under her chin, she took a bite, then another, and when she didn't want a third, she consented to lick a gob of tuna from my fingers.

"That's one end accounted for and in working order," I told Linda. "Now let's hope the other end still works."

As her appetite increased, we began examining her cookie-sheet litter box for any evidence of use. No prospector ever scrutinized his pan for grains of gold more closely than we squinted over her litter. A week after her accident, she had regained enough mobility to shift position on her carton-top pillow, but we had never seen her move off it. Not even an accidental visit from Agnes prompted her to stir. I caught our black cat snuffling around Frannie's litter tray after I had left the door open to refill her water bowl. Neither cat acted as if she had seen the other, and Agnes scampered back upstairs to resume her second-story exile.

Frannie may have had her rough-and-tumble uncivilized aspects, but she proved to be scrupulous in her bathroom eti-quette. Even though she couldn't walk, in the middle of the night she somehow managed to inch herself over to the litter box, use it with the utmost neatness, and crawl back to her pillow again. I doubt that any human being in the entirety of human history had ever been as excited to clean kitty litter as I was the following morning.

AGNES DIDN'T TAKE long to turn Frannie's injury to her benefit. Although she had only nosed around the porch for a minute or two, she had worked out the mathematics of the situation. Adding Frannie's immobile carriage to Frannie's subtraction from the rest of the house, Agnes began dividing her day between the upstairs and the basement. The inevitable moment arrived when she bleated at the door to go out. I thought up several reasons against it. None of them convinced me in the end, considering that Agnes had spent almost as much time outdoors as indoors over the last thirteen years. She had come to us as a stray just like Frannie and boasted far more street smarts than I'd ever have. So I opened the door.

I watched her as she became queen of the world. She streaked between the pine trees. She made the wind blow through the weeds. She dug holes in Linda's vegetable garden, climbed the gate post, fled from the geese, soaked up every inch of daylight, and brought out Venus dangling low on the horizon. I didn't know if Frannie envied her, lying on her pillow on her cardboard box top, but I did. I needed to go outside. I needed to escape from worry. I needed to run to the river with Agnes flying behind me.

"You need to go on your little trip with Bill," said Linda.

Just the thought of the yellow-headed blackbird, half midnight, half blazing sunshine, put a half smile on my face.

Bill had phoned the ranger's office at Nayanquing Point State Wildlife Area and learned that this was probably the final week if we wanted to see the yellow-headed blackbird. After that, the handful of courting males would stop singing, sink behind the cattails, and disappear.

"Frannie can take of herself now," Linda said.

• • •

WE SHUDDERED DOWN a deeply rutted gravel road. The weeds that brushed the Volvo Bill had named Turbo were so high, we might as well have been driving through a tunnel. I asked Bill to turn off the CD. He was playing *Buddy Ebsen Says Howdy* to annoy me, and I needed to listen for birds. "You don't want to enjoy 'Everything's Okay' one more time? It's my new theme song." Buzzes, zips, and trills swirled past us in a rush of heat when I rolled down the window.

"So, that's your philosophy?" I shouted above the tire noise. "Everything's okay?"

He rolled up my window. "My what?"

"You told me twice you had a philosophy of life, or happiness, or something." Sunlight blanked out the screen of the GPS, which didn't recognize the road we were on anyway. It showed the icon of a car in empty space.

"I guess it's to just let things happen, more or less."

"Kind of a Zen thing?" I asked. "Living in the present moment? That sort of thing?"

"God, no. Anything but the present moment. I avoid it at all costs."

We reached a wide spot at the end of the road near the observation tower. I'd brought a hat this time. Last year we had trudged around the cattail ponds for hours in heat that sapped our wits, leaving us no wiser and no closer to the yellow-headed blackbird. This year we were better prepared for the grueling hike that was exactly what I needed to derail my anxiety over Frannie.

"Give me your water bottle." He fitted it into a survival belt bulging with loops and pockets that he had grabbed from the backseat, then he wrestled his field guide into the belt. "I've got organic blueberries and fair-trade peanuts in case we work up a mighty hunger." He flung open the door. "Anything else we need?"

"Yeah, luck."

The plan was to climb the tower and pick a starting point for our search. As Bill's survival belt slipped off, I heard what sounded like a red-winged blackbird as interpreted by Buddy Ebsen. "Yellow-headed blackbird," I gasped. It was shockingly beautiful, grafting the brilliant head of a yellow warbler onto the body of a cowbird.

"Isn't that one?" asked Bill, pointing to a second patch of weeds less than twenty feet from the car. "Sitting with a female?"

But after that, it was all anticlimactic as we hiked the ponds. We surprised a trio of black-crowned night herons that barked like dogs, watched a northern harrier conduct its ghostly glide in search of prey, and heckled the eastern kingbirds that shadowed us. But our peak experience had long since faded. I couldn't get Frannie off my mind and wanted to go home.

FRANNIE WAS STILL box-top bound when I got back. I had only seen her up on her feet that one time, and I was starting to wonder if a three-legged hobble was as good as it would get. I had met dogs and cats that navigated quite nimbly as tripods, so Frannie could certainly learn to cope without the use of one leg. But I could tell that her lack of progress frustrated her. Being an invalid was bringing out the Lucy side of her personality.

Maybe she was sick of hearing about the yellow-headed blackbird. I was telling her that the blackbird was the most beautiful bird that I had ever seen, "but my little girl is even prettier," when she whacked my hand with her front paw. Thinking that she required a treat to elevate her mood, I microwaved a dollop of fancy cat food. It had come in a microscopic can and cost more per ounce than opium.

Back on the porch, I was shocked to find her planted in front of me on the welcome mat standing on all four legs. I didn't want her crossing paths with queen of the world Agnes, who had sidled up behind me in hopes of sharing the food. The resumption of warfare didn't strike me as the best recuperative strategy.

Without thinking I clapped my hands to disperse the opposing generals—a stupid thing to do. A startled Agnes flew up the stairs. Limping but moving assuredly, Frannie scurried across the porch and vaulted up to the windowsill. While I was thrilled that she had rejoined the quadruped club, she had gone one hurdle too far for my peace of mind. Moobie's bathroom-vanity gymnastics had caused me enough grief already. I didn't need a second feeble cat trying to break an Olympic record and who knew what else.

I lifted Frannie off the sill to set her down on her box-top bed. But just as she loved to be petted while she ate, she now apparently associated her accident with being carried. She clung to my ribcage as if it were a tree trunk as she squeaked pathetically. I touched her down on the floor and she trotted over to her cardboard box, while I retreated to the bathroom to examine several puncture wounds.

"Where's Agnes?" I asked Linda as I held the doorknob.

"Outside taking a chipmunk census."

"Kitchen door closed?"

She nodded. "But that gate isn't going to do any good. Frannie will fly right over it."

"Not with a bum hip." I checked the "baby gate" at the foot of the stairs. "It's enough to discourage her."

"Until she breathes on it and knocks it over," Linda said.

Thanks to the nurturing effects of the stream of worry I directed toward Frannie, she was walking more smoothly and less like a windup toy soldier every day. We didn't want any hitches in her recovery, so we confined her to a single room at a time to reduce the temptation to rocket around at high speeds. And above all we kept her away from a certain cantankerous cat.

The cantankerous cat had other plans. I let Frannie in, and while I fiddled with the gate, Agnes darted out from behind the rocking chair and charged at Frannie. Frannie stumbled backward, seemingly cowed. Then she stiffened her front legs and slingshotted herself at Agnes to the music of a growl from deep inside her chest. Agnes leaped over the gate, banging it with her foot. Frannie followed, sailing over it like an Olympic hurdler, chasing Agnes into the upstairs bedroom.

That victory seemed to stimulate the healing process. To our amazement the limp all but vanished within a couple of weeks, the better for Frannie to pace back and forth in front of doors.

"I don't want her going outside again," I said. "I'll worry about her every minute."

"I know, but she isn't happy in the house," Linda said. "And we really don't know what happened to her. Didn't the vet say that she might have fallen from a tree? We can't keep her away from everything."

I didn't like it, but I knew that Linda was right. Frannie was a stray who needed her space. So after agonizing about it for a while, I threw open the exit.

To her credit, she changed her behavior. On the plus side, she no longer vanished into the woods for hours at a time. Following Lucy's example, she clung to the periphery of the house, snoozing on the picnic table, stretching out on a sunny patch of lawn, or sitting contentedly on the cement steps. On the negative side, she had made up her mind to be more resistant than ever about coming back inside.

AFTER DINNER, ONCE I had lured the ducks and geese into the barn with table scraps, I opened the basement door for Frannie, who had been trotting along at my heels. Instead of following me into the house, she rubbed back and forth against the door frame. Then, making certain that I was watching, she pranced over to caress a picnic table leg. I returned a few minutes later with a chunk of warm chicken on a plate. A dance ensued that brought her an inch inside the open door before she pirouetted and skittered back to the picnic table. When I walked over to her, she trotted away.

"She's hardly been outdoors for weeks," I told Linda. "I'll give her another half hour."

She performed the door frame–rubbing routine twice more. When it got to be eight thirty, she had parked herself less than three feet from the basement door but farther away from coming inside than ever. The more I wheedled her, the more coquettish she became. "That's enough," I told her. "You've got to come in. Or you're not going out again for a very long time." She let me get within inches of grabbing her—I was angry enough to violate our no-picking-up-the-cat understanding—when she dashed under the pine tree, reappearing to tease me with the lovable kitty blink, which stung. It was a desecration of that blink that she had given me at the emergency clinic.

"How could she treat me this way after everything I've done for her?" I asked Linda, sounding remarkably like a sit-com parent. I made one final attempt to coerce Frannie in, but she wouldn't even poke her nose out from under the tree.

A little after nine o'clock, as I settled in for a long night's journey into anxiety, Linda announced that the cat who had made a mousie toy out of me was at the side door scratching to come in. On the porch, I fed her in silence, banged the door shut, and peered out through the living room window as she hopped up onto her box to lick her feet.

"You can't really expect anything else from Frannie," Linda said as we got into bed. "She already traded a lot of her freedom for the security of living with us, and since her accident, she's given up even more."

I didn't say a word. If I couldn't argue with Frannie, I could give Linda the cold shoulder for her taking her side. I was about to pull up the covers and turn toward the wall, but I relented and kissed her good night instead.

I loved each of our cats, even the next-to-impossible-to-love Lucy, but Frannie struck me as special. Her virtues wouldn't impress most people. She lacked Moobie's friendly personality, Agnes bettered her in the feistiness department, and Lucy was second to none as a chair hogger, to give credit where credit was due. Even our duck Victor was more affectionate. Frannie could be quirky, twitchy, fearful, proud, manipulative—no, wait a minute, that was me. There was a deep and possibly pathological bond between us, making me feel like she was the kind of cat that came along just once in a lifetime.

CHAPTER 10

Don't Call Him "Mr. Cuddle-Wuddle"

Months later Frannie was still wary of us. The mere threat of being petted as she waited at the door elicited a pitiful *eek*. And when I tapped the floor and urged in a falsetto voice, "Come see me, sweetie," I might as well have been talking to a cactus. Lucy, of all cats, answered by hopping onto the couch and hooking one paw over my knee, despite the lack of pine tar–based shampoo. Frannie was now officially the most standoffish member of the household.

I phoned my sister Joan for encouragement, expecting to hear that her feral cat Ember had lived up to her name by warming up to them.

"We can't touch her," she said. "Not if we don't want to get shredded. She likes being around us, and we can play with her with a string. But she's not a cat you can touch."

"How did you ever take her to the vet to get her spayed?"

"I bought a pair of heavy leather gloves that covered my arm up to the elbow. Then I put on my thickest winter coat and lowered her into a pet carrier as quickly as I could."

Joan's experience sounded like way more adventure than I could handle at the moment. As I lay down in the mattress for a nap, Moobie settled in alongside me for the first time in weeks. She had shrunken in both mass and energy and spent her days curled up on a pile of clothes in our closet. I had missed her, and it depressed me to realize that I'd probably never have this kind of physical closeness with Frannie. But at least I could touch her without fear of getting shredded.

Linda interrupted my nap to tell me that her friend Reverend Evans couldn't care for his cat any longer because of his Parkinson's disease. Could we take him? Word had apparently percolated up from the stray-cat grapevine to human clerical circles that we were pushovers for feline orphans.

If the call had come through while Frannie was recuperating, I wouldn't have just said no. I would have snipped the phone cord. As it happened, we were enjoying an extraordinary phase when none of our animals was causing us any trouble. Yes, Bella had bitten me when I had handed her a peanut, and the cord to the dining room radio near Rudy the rabbit's cage was missing a strip of insulation. But no parakeet, parrot, dove, rabbit, goose, hen, or cat was currently ill or injured—and Linda hadn't seen another bear. So as I furrowed my brow and pretended to be occupied in thought, I was actually stifling a yawn. Our animals suddenly seemed so effortless to live with that keeping a mineral healthy would be exhausting in comparison. I couldn't come up with an argument against taking in another cat. But I still told her, "No. Four cats is enough." I didn't want to disturb a perfect state of equilibrium.

"He's eight years old," Linda said. "He won't be able to find another home and will have to go to the animal shelter."

"Good. Then Lucy will have company." I also ignored her insistence that this was a lap cat who loved people. *Very affectionate,* I could hear her saying next. Instead she dropped a bombshell that blew away my objections.

"His name is Mabel. They thought he was a girl when he was a kitten, so they called him Mabel and they never changed his name."

"You mean to tell me —" I could barely speak through my indignation. "You're saying that for eight years this male cat has been saddled with a girl's name?"

"I don't know why they didn't change it, but that's what Reverend Evans told me."

I just *knew* this had to be emblematic of a long history of neglect. I envisioned a sad-eyed cat, naked except for a few stray tufts of hair and scrawny enough that he could slip through the bars of Bella's cage.

"Get the poor guy over here," I said. I hoped we weren't too late.

FRANNIE MUST HAVE overheard Linda's phone conversation with Reverend Evans. She registered her displeasure by climbing a tree and stationing herself on a branch twenty feet off the ground. A robin was singing from the redbud tree, drowning out her low-octane squeak, but I could see her mouth opening and closing.

"She's trying to get down, but she can't figure out how to do it," Linda said. Turning around on the branch to face the trunk, Frannie inched forward until she was vertical, head pointed downward. As gravity grabbed her, she hopped down to a lower branch, which seemed like progress. But there were no more branches beneath her. Turning logic on its head, she climbed back up to her former perch and then ascended to the next branch up. She stared down at us and opened her mouth.

"Call Gary," Linda said. Gary was our handyman and a good friend who happened to be a sucker for animals, especially cats.

"They usually come down on their own," Gary told me on the phone, reacting to my hysteria with typical calm. "It might take a while."

"I'm worried about her leg. It's permanently dislocated, and I don't know what will happen if she falls. And I don't know what kind of shape her pelvis is in."

Twenty minutes later he was leveling his ladder against the tree. I didn't want to mention it, but I felt obligated to interrupt his climb with advice. "She doesn't like being picked up, and she isn't declawed. So you might want to be careful."

"I'll do my best," he said. "I've gotten scratched lots of times." Frannie must have watched a sitcom depiction of cat behavior in a tree, because she initially climbed down toward Gary, but just as he stepped within arm's length, she scrambled higher. "I could wait up here awhile," he said. He was on the third rung from the top. "I really can't do much else."

"It's going to be too dark to see her soon," said Linda.

After fifteen minutes of wheedling her, Gary called it a night. "She'll come down," he said. "She'll get hungry by morning." We thanked him profusely, though I felt wounded that he hadn't worked a miracle.

I caught cell-less Gary on his landline just as he walked into the house. "As soon as you left," I told him, "I looked out the window and she was prancing around in the grass. You wouldn't even know that anything had happened." I knew something had happened, though. The surge of adrenaline kept me up for hours. I spent the time wondering what kind of trouble Mabel would bring.

THE EXPRESSIONS OF the two men in our front hallway activated my naughty-cat radar. Linda introduced me to the soft-spoken Reverend Evans, whose gentlemanly demeanor reminded me of my late dad, and his son, Paul, a college professor who appeared fit enough to bench-press me. I took a step backward toward the stairs in case that thought occurred to him. I noticed that Mabel hadn't accompanied them inside.

"The cat's still in the car," Linda said.

"In the backseat, last time we saw him," Paul chimed in. Both he and his dad smiled helpfully, but neither of them moved.

"Is he in a carrier?" They traded glances and shook their heads, nope, no carrier. Reverend Evans grinned in apparent appreciation of the idea of pet carriers in general. Neither of them had budged, though their faces brimmed with encouragement.

"Would you like me to get him?" I asked. Paul nodded his approval. "Could I just carry Mabel in my arms?"

"You could try," he said, "but he might bite you."

"He's quite the cat," Reverend Evans said with a chuckle.

Linda told them that Mabel would have to be nice to Moobie, Frannie, and Lucy if he wanted to live with us. (Agnes' name didn't even come up.) Paul reassured her that Mabel didn't really bite all that much as a rule. Reverend Evans agreed, and the two men expressed the opinion that it would definitely be a good thing if people's cats got along. As they drifted into the living room and farther from the cat in the car, the discussion meandered away from Mabel and toward animals in general—backyard birds, the crazy things that squirrels did. I understood that I couldn't put off the inevitable any longer unless I called Joan and asked to borrow her gloves that went all the way up to the elbow. I ducked into the basement for a pet carrier, and then I announced, "I guess we should go out and get him." Fortified by supportive nods, I marched toward their car. The faces in the window were solidly behind me.

I WASN'T A brave man. But I had the benefit of ignorance. I knew that there were cats like Ember who would shred you if you touched them, but they existed as far outside of my personal experience as a can-do attitude. So I resolved to make a stab at getting Mabel into the carrier.

I cautiously opened the rear driver's side door—and froze. Gazing up at me from the floor was the silliest cat I had ever seen. He emitted a long meow that resembled a moan of complaint from our hen Helen. Normally I considered animals to be my betters. I'd rarely met a dog, cat, bird, or swine that didn't brandish some trait I envied, and I'd learned to respect the defenses of a creature as small as a three-inch-long short-tailed shrew. But I had never felt more equal to and less intimidated by any living creature than Mabel. His classic gray American tabby markings would have lent a strikingly handsome flash to any other cat. But the cream-colored circles edged in black around his eyes, his white chin and muzzle, and the dramatic M on his forehead collided with a goofy expression to give him the air of a Mardi Gras clown. He meowed again mournfully. I hesitated to pick him up, concerned that he might make me laugh so hard that I would drop him.

The great big beanbag complained as I eased him into the

carrier, but he didn't seem unusually put out by what he considered to be another of life's travails. "Didn't put up much of a fight?" Paul asked as I opened the carrier door and the cat slipped behind the entertainment center. When I squatted down, Mabel peered back as if we had known each other for years and I had disappointed him yet again.

As Linda peppered Paul with a flurry of questions about his students at the college, he and his father slowly, almost imperceptibly, reversed direction from the center of the room until the minister had curled his fingers around the doorknob. "Sarah's going to miss him," he told me. I heartily agreed, *no doubt about it, she sure will,* while shooting Linda a "Who's Sarah?" glance. Reverend Evans pumped my hand and thanked me as we walked them to the car.

"It must be hard for him to give up his cat when he lives alone," I said.

"I didn't know it wasn't his cat," said Linda.

"What do you mean? Whose cat is he?"

"I only took him because I thought he belonged to Reverend Evans. His daughter Sarah's new boyfriend doesn't like cats, so Reverend Evans was looking after Mabel for her until she could find a home for him."

This news flabbergasted me. We turned down "take my cat" pleas all of the time from friends, and now a priceless slot in our house had been scarfed up by a stranger—and for what I considered to be the worst of all reasons for getting rid of a kitty. I would have chucked out the boyfriend instead.

None of this changed the fact that Mabel needed a home. But as he ratcheted up his meows a dozen decibels, I doubted that the home would be with us.

THE REVEREND HAD spoken God's own truth when he told Linda that Mabel was a lap cat. Concerned that he might hide behind the entertainment center all day and run afoul of Frannie when she came back inside, I sat on the rug and made soothing comments to lure him closer. I had barely begun when he lumbered out and slumped down onto my lap.

My heart was gratified by his demonstration of trust and affection. My legs held a contrary opinion. As I petted him and he began to purr, the blood pooled in my thighs. Mabel wasn't fat like Lucy. He was solid, not squishy—a propane tank wrapped in fur. I called Linda into the room to witness this spectacle of an unusually sweet kitty and also to help me back up on my feet, since I had lost all feeling below the knees. As I leaned against the wall struggling to regain my balance, Mabel meowed for more, conveying his judgment that no cat on the planet had ever been so ill-used.

"There's an awfully nice big boy," Linda told him. His answering yowl was unsettlingly strident. She stooped down and started petting him.

Judging her petting too halfhearted, he butted her calf with his head as a prelude to crashing down onto his side and rattling the floorboards. He glared up at her expectantly. When she slapped his ample rear end appreciably and began to walk away, he yowled an unmistakable, *No!* A flicker of eye contact passed between Linda and me, but we both pretended we hadn't heard our newest child utter his first naughty word.

Linda got the jump on me by exiting the room first. I tried to give Mabel the slip by scurrying upstairs, but he stayed on my trail, bawling as he whisked past a surprised Agnes, then sticking with me as I doubled back and ran down the stairs two at a time. I shut myself inside the bedroom, but the caterwauling outside the door was worse than having him at my feet. I let him in and he hopped up onto the bed, banging into my hip and knocking me off balance. He tossed himself down like a professional wrestler thrown by an invisible opponent. As soon as I touched him, his desperate breathing slowed to a pulsing purr. As soon as I stopped, he snapped to his feet and demanded more.

"Aren't cats supposed to be shy and retiring when you first get them?" I asked Linda. I began to appreciate what Reverend Evans and his son had gone through on their fifty-mile trip to our house.

AGNES TRAIPSED DOWNSTAIRS to snarl at the noise source, received a plea for understanding from Mabel in reply, and raced back up to the safety of my office chair. I didn't expect any problems between Mabel and Frannie, since Frannie had adjusted easily to living with Lucy and Moobie. But I was wrong again. She turned into a white-and-black bundle of nerves clawing the woodwork and demanding entry to the porch. She pushed through as I opened the door, bounded up on top of her cardboard box, and compacted herself into a defensive posture. When Mabel followed she streaked past him and cringed behind the bed.

I couldn't figure out what she had seen in the oversized infant of a cat that could have terrified her. Then I realized it was what she had heard. His meow resembled the stray tabby's declaration of love during Frannie's first night with us. Shushing Mabel, I sat on the rug next to the bed and cooed at Frannie, but that only succeeded in pushing her deeper into the shadows.

AFTER FIVE DAYS of Mabel's whining, Linda couldn't take it anymore. She met me at the door in such a state of exasperation that I looked around the porch for a cardboard tube from a nursery. "I talked to Mabel's owner, Sarah, today. She described him as 'needy' and said he'd always been that way. Needy? He's a basket case. She said he was fine if you just sit and pet him. I've got fifty animals to care for, and you can only get so much work done petting a cat all day."

"How's Frannie?" I asked.

"Frannie's fine as long as she's outdoors. I'm stuck in the house. He needs to find some owner who has all the time in the world. I put an ad in the *Ledger,* saying, 'extremely friendly, babyish cat, kind of loud,' and I told Reverend Evans that we can't keep him."

"We won't give him away unless we find the perfect person," I said.

Linda shut her eyes. "The perfect person would be anyone who would take him."

I had forgotten that placing a classified newspaper ad for a cat was equivalent to casting an invisibility spell on us. All phone calls, mail delivery, and e-mails ceased—except for a sympathetic Nigerian scammer who said he'd take our cat if we took ten of his. None of our friends noticed me when I wheeled my cart alongside them at the store up the street. On the plus side, the Aisle Blockers allowed me unimpeded access to glittering shelves of toothpaste, work gloves, hose fittings, and artichoke hearts.

While we waited to blink back into existence, we thought we might calm Mabel down by giving him a gender-appropriate name. We had always waited for a new pet's name to pop into our heads even if it took weeks, but this was an emergency. "*Maynard* sounds enough like *Mabel* that he probably won't know the difference," I said—and his laziness in between wailing expeditions reminded me of Bob Denver's work-avoiding beatnik Maynard G. Krebs in *The Many Loves of Dobie Gillis* sitcom. So Maynard he became—just in time for a prospective owner to visit. Someone had actually answered Linda's ad.

ALTHOUGH MAYNARD'S NAME change hadn't subdued his existential angst, his whining didn't trouble Nana, whose old-world brusqueness matched her name. "Is that as loud as he gets? *Pfft.* That's nothing. I thought you were talking about *loud.*"

"It may get on your nerves when he does it all day," Linda said.

"Things like that don't get on my nerves," she snapped, raising her shoulders and lurching toward him to the accompaniment of a kissing sound. "I know all about cats," she swung around to tell me as Maynard hightailed it into the bedroom.

"Did you bring a pet carrier? We can lend you one."

"I came to look at him first, because I was told he was loud." She looked accusingly at Linda. "I'll take him. Tomorrow I'll buy dishes and a litter box, then I'll come back for him." I wanted to offer her all the bowls and litter boxes she could carry if she took him now, but I didn't want to disturb the rhythm of a sale so easily made. "Good-bye, cat," she said, ducking her head into the bedroom and treating Maynard to another smooching sound. She brought her full mass to a halt on our welcome mat and sought reassurance on one point. "You're sure he's friendly?"

"He's a big baby," Linda said. "He likes nothing better than to be petted all day."

"Let me see," she said. As she swept into the bedroom, Linda and I blocked the open door behind us in case Maynard decided to bolt. Draped across Linda's pillow, he looked especially cuddly-wuddly. "Cats always like me," she told us. "Kitty, kitty." She pitched forward onto the bed and thrust her head into his face, grabbing him. He responded just as I would have. He nipped at her hand. "That's nasty," she said.

"He just doesn't know you yet," Linda said.

"You are a very nasty cat," she told him. "I don't mind the loud, but I don't like the nasty. He's not for me." As she left, I wondered if every event in her life was initiated and concluded this quickly. It was possible that she had literally been born yesterday.

"The ad runs another two days," said Linda. But we both knew this had been our one and only chance. Maynard had flaunted his newly minted masculinity at the worst possible time.

LINDA WAS SENSITIVE to sounds—not to mention smells, temperature variations, and swallowing any size pill—and Maynard was remarkably, disconcertingly loud. His attention-seeking wails were stolen from the playbook of a toddler in the candy aisle. Still, I was surprised to see my softhearted wife turn a stony side to an animal.

"I don't care how we do it, but he's got to go," she told me.

"Don't you think he's been a tiny bit better lately?" That earned me the same glare that she gave Maynard. "I think he's a little bit quieter than when we first got him," I said. Helping me out, he erupted in a series of yowls. Linda snatched up the washcloths she'd been folding and strode into the dining room, seeking the comparatively quiet scream of an African grey parrot.

I was more forgiving. Ever since Moobie had relocated her daytime operations to the back of the closet, Maynard had stepped up to fill the nap gap.

As I lay on my back, the yodeler crashed down between my arm and ribcage, tail tucked into my armpit. When I awoke twenty minutes later, I hugged the purring hulk against me. "You're just a regular Mr. Cuddle-Wuddle," I told him. He gave a clipped yelp and swiveled his ears backward. "Mr. Cuddle-Wuddle," I cooed a second time. Insulted, he fled the room.

Later that afternoon, when I returned from my daily trip to the store for some item I'd forgotten to buy the day before—fruit for the parrots, lettuce for the ducks, gingersnaps for the wife—I caught the wife speaking in conciliatory tones to Maynard. "What's the matter with the great big boy?"

She explained, "I just got off the phone with Lori Koster." Lori lived a few miles away and took in unwanted cats, so I concluded that Linda had found him a new home. "She used to have a real pest of a cat who followed her around meowing all the time, just like you-know-who. He suddenly got sick and died, and she ended up missing him much more than she missed her cats who weren't so noisy."

"He does have his nice side."

"I've been closing him in the upstairs bedroom every morning to keep my sanity. If I forget, he whines and makes me follow him upstairs. It gives both of us a break."

Linda called his former owner, Sarah, to let her know that

we were keeping him, which is when she learned something about his past that helped seal the deal. "Sarah used to have a second, much older cat named Sam, and he and Maynard had been inseparable buddies," Linda told me. "They always slept cuddled up with one another. Sam died, and that's when he got worse about his meowing."

FRANNIE BORE THE brunt of Maynard's attempt to reprise the intimacy that he'd lost. The more she ran away from him, the more ardently he pursued her. She became more jittery than ever, projecting herself across the room if any human or cat came within six feet. Her ears swiveled to track sounds, like miniature satellite dishes. Linda clomping into a room in her usual plate-rattling manner would send Frannie scurrying for cover. Even Moobie's ghostly glide into a room blasted her nerve endings. But a confrontation between Agnes and Maynard soon eased her fears.

Maynard had been bleating to hop up onto my lap as I sat at the computer upstairs. Accommodating smallish Agnes on my lap as I tried to peck away at my keyboard was difficult enough. With Maynard, it was impossible. He spilled from my legs onto the desk. "No way," I said and was on the verge of shooing him downstairs when Agnes beat me to it. Popping out from under the metal typewriter table, she pursued him in a snarling fit of possessiveness all the way down to the first-floor bedroom.

Frannie witnessed the routing of Maynard from the front

hallway. I didn't know if she possessed a logical facility that most cats lacked or she simply processed what she had seen: the cat who chased her (Maynard) was being chased by the cat (Agnes) that Frannie usually chased. No hen would have tolerated such a breach in the pecking order, and neither did Frannie. The next time that Maynard barged whining into her personal space, a clawed correction sent him toddling back toward the humans.

As Maynard grew more secure with us, he scaled down his discontent. Although he remained a "Grade-A" nuisance, he let enough time elapse between his worst outbursts that we could describe him as talkative rather than impossible. As we began to appreciate his boisterous expressions of affection — and snuggly quiet during nap time — we came to view Nana's visit as a close call that would have robbed us of a friend.

"That woman didn't deserve such a nice cat," Linda said. "I wonder if he knew what was going on and acted bad on purpose." I doubted it, though I believed with equal conviction that anything was possible with a cat.

"If only Frannie would notice how happy Maynard is on my lap and take the hint," I said.

But his example didn't convince her to approach me. I consoled myself by remembering Joan's cat Ember and understanding that every kitty didn't have to show its love in a touchy-feely manner. I could hug and paw Maynard to my heart's content—as long as I restrained myself from uttering the dreaded name. Sometimes the temptation was too great to resist.

Linda was lying on her faux-sheepskin rug on the floor with Maynard plastered against her side as the closing credits rolled to *Charlie Chan at Treasure Island*. Creeping across the room on my hands and knees, I tousled the big loud log of a cat. "Do you have a special name?" He scrambled to his feet with a yelp. "Are you my Mr. Cuddle-Wuddle?" Right on cue, he tore up the steps and hid under the bed. We figured that he associated the tone of voice with someone in his past getting uncomfortably in his face, a phobia that Nana had accidentally tapped into.

The insult was forgotten by the following afternoon when he bounded onto the mattress. And as I lay stock-still flirting with sleep, I heard a soft scrabbling beside me on the floor between the bed and wall. Out of the corner of my eye I caught a hint of white and black, but I didn't dare turn my head. Too shy for actual intimacy, Frannie had substituted proximity by stretching out on the floor for a vicariously shared snooze. It was a huge step.

"Frannie," I whispered.

She was gone instantly, but the glow of her presence remained.

CHAPTER 11

. . . .

The Anti-Frannie

As I complained to Linda about a recent snubbing from Frannie, I saw myself writ large in our big baby of a cat. Even more embarrassing, I started to view all of our cats as feline personifications of my shortcomings. Moobie's incessant wanting, Agnes' crabbiness, and Lucy's sense of entitlement made me feel like the protagonist in a kitty version of *The Pilgrim's Progress,* with fresh lessons on how not to live lurking in every litter box.

Frannie's stubbornness had set me off when I couldn't find her as a storm of biblical proportions rolled in. The talking moose weather radio had fibbed that the afternoon would be partly cloudy. When the fully cloudy sky turned a sickly yellow, Linda hurried in from the backyard. I stood in the basement door hollering for Miss Ferret Face. The first blast of wind sent our pair of $4.99 plastic lawn chairs cartwheeling across the lawn. Thunder crackled in the distance. I popped open the basement door a second time expecting Frannie to shoot inside. But she wasn't there.

Galloping out in pursuit of a vinyl patio table, I checked for her behind the wheelbarrow and then stuck my head under the pine boughs where she usually hung out. Our geese honked in apprehension. After checking the perimeter of the house, I ran toward the barn into a sheet of gloom, calling for her all the way. "Frannie! You're going to get wet!" Our neighbor's gravel driveway came alive, spattering me with mud as the waterworks erupted. Leaves tore loose and swirled in the air. Branches clattered above my head. I started toward the river but was driven back by a wind that nearly picked me up off my feet. At that point, I couldn't have seen or heard Frannie if she had been trotting along at my heels.

Linda and I met at the basement door, where we performed an impromptu Three Stooges routine trying to get into the house at the same time. She had also been shouting for Frannie and was even more soaked than I was. "I'm worried about her," I said.

"Oh, you know cats," she said. "They manage to find shelter somewhere and come out after it stops raining without a wet hair on their bodies." As I hung up my jacket, I glanced down to see Frannie lying on a pile of bedding next to the basement refrigerator. She had never been outdoors at all.

"You heard us calling you," I scolded. "Over and over and over again. You could have come out and let us know that you were okay." Frannie treated me to her innocent kitty blink and didn't stir from the bedding.

"Can't we have just one normal cat?"

"That *is* normal for a cat," Linda said.

I thought of what Bill Holm had told me the last time I groused to him about how crazy and complicated Frannie was. "That's because they're people, only smarter. They know us better than we know them, and a lot of them have a sense of humor. They're exactly like us minus our useless mental power and thumbs."

LATER THAT WEEK, Linda called to me from the porch. "You should see this sweet little kitty. She's barely older than a kitten, but she's already a mother." I was catted out. I had no intention of heaving myself to my feet, crossing an entire room, and poking my nose into the porch to look at a cat that didn't belong to us.

Pastor Larry from Linda's church had phoned with an odd request. He had driven twenty-one miles from Ionia to see a movie with his son and daughter-in-law, Nicole, who fostered cats. Before enjoying *Buck Benny Rides Again, Steamboat Bill, Jr.,* or whatever it was that was playing, they had planned on dropping off a mother cat and her kittens for shots at the vet down the street. But Dr. LeBlanc put the youngsters on his scale and determined that they didn't weigh enough yet to get poked with needles. So Pastor Larry asked Linda if we could take the cats for a couple of hours while they watched

Song of the Thin Man, My Man Godfrey, or possibly *Bringing Up Baby.*

"I don't like the idea of them sitting in the carrier the whole time," Linda told me. "But we're not supposed to let them out. They haven't been tested for anything."

"I'm not looking at them," I said.

She trotted back out to the porch to check on the cats and returned to continue a running commentary about how precious they were. "The mother keeps looking at me with the most appealing expression. She has this peaceful and gentle demeanor. Come see her. She's just the picture of feminine grace and tenderness."

"I'm in a really good part of this book and I don't want to put it down right now."

These weren't simply adorable cats, of course. These were adorable cats in need of a home, and I recognized the danger of getting anywhere close to them. While Linda had already been contaminated by their cuteness, I could still keep my distance so that at least one of us didn't catch the adoption bug. Unfortunately, the disorder was extremely contagious. As Linda went on and on about what a nice influence a sweet, calm cat would be on Maynard, I caught myself saying, "Maybe if he had a friend, he wouldn't act so needy." It had come out of me like a sneeze before I could stop it.

I trudged out to take a gander at the cat that I had apparently just agreed to take.

As I reached into the carrier and petted the white-and-caramel-colored cat, I wasn't thinking about Maynard, who had been howling since I abandoned him and my book. Frannie came to mind. She couldn't have been more different from the contented and self-assured mother. As the youngster huddled with her kittens, calm as a blade of grass, our Alfalfa girl patrolled the backyard terrorizing the local wildlife.

"Is that even the same cat?" I asked Linda a few weeks later as I slammed and locked the porch door behind me. "That can't be the peaceful little mother cat."

"She's about as peaceful as the Hardy Boys."

The white-and-caramel-colored cat seemed much tinier to me now—a kitten who had given birth to kittens. And her personality had undergone a shocking change. Nicole had kept her for three weeks while weaning the babies, then another two weeks treating her with antibiotics to kill some internal bug. I theorized that the drug must have flipped the poles of the magnetically charged particles orbiting her chromosomes that were responsible for her previous calm demeanor. Linda had a more prosaic explanation; her former placidity was a hormone-induced state that had kept her attentive to her kittens. Once she stopped nursing the babies, she reverted to a maniac.

"I'm not letting her inside. Frannie won't mind losing the porch for a little while," I said without consulting Frannie.

The kitten's enormous energy reserves fueled a darting shyness that sent her flying beneath the mound of jackets

that disguised our coatrack. Our interactions with her consisted of equal parts examining whatever object she had just
knocked off a shelf and cajoling her to approach us. "It's okay,"
I told her in response to the latest teeth-jarring crash. "Linda
didn't need a photo printer anyway." If I kept up the reassuring chatter from a bench on the opposite end of the porch,
she eventually jackrabbited over to absorb a volley of petting
before retreating to her hidey-hole to plan the next destruc-
tive bit of fun.

Once we had removed everything of value from the porch
except the exercise bike, she occupied her time carving her
initials into the front door. Her name had come to me at once.
"Teeny-weeny Tina's up to no good again," I told Linda.

"Did you just think that up? You must have heard me call
her Tina this morning."

I shook my head. "Tina Louise. Ginger on *Gilligan's Island.*
She's kind of ginger colored and way too cute for her own
good." That cuteness compensated for a wealth of naughtiness. I hated to admit it, but I no longer considered Frannie to
be the most irresistible kitty in the world. Pudgy Tina with her
searchlight eyes, lopsided slit of a questioning mouth, and a tail
that she carried straight up and crooked forward, periscope-
style, was so addictively adorable that I couldn't keep my
hands off her. And that led to problems with Frannie.

Lucy, Frannie, and Maynard were all nervous when
they first came into the house. So I stuck close to Tina as I

opened the door. But instead of proceeding cautiously, she immediately made the worst decision possible.

I bounded behind her as she shot upstairs into Agnes' territory. A rising growl from across the room stopped her at the landing. Before I could rescue her, Agnes launched a ferocious snarling charge that brought her to within an inch of Tina, but Tina didn't even flinch. She stood her ground, stretching her neck to get a good whiff of the fire and brimstone hissing from Agnes' throat. Still growling, Agnes backed away. She turned on her kitty heels and skulked off under the bed trying to figure out what had just happened.

I wanted to join her. After living with Moobie for so long, I had developed a high tolerance for pestering. With two rabbits and two parrots in the house, I had also developed some immunity to chaos. But Tina created a new flavor of disruption. We needed to watch her constantly to keep her from laying waste to everything we owned.

We had recently gotten rid of our entertainment center, replacing it with a squatty cabinet that held our new flat-screen television. The baby shoe of a base that supported the TV didn't inspire confidence, but in the earthquake-free zone where we lived, it seemed stable enough. We weren't located in a Tina-free zone, however.

I was keeping one eye on a Sherlock Holmes movie and the other eye on Tina, when she jumped up onto the cabinet and stalked back and forth between the TV and the wall. Our TV wobbled and shuddered as she nudged it, providing the

nail-biting suspense that *Dressed to Kill* lacked. No sooner had
I shooed her off than I heard outraged squawks from parakeet
Harvey. I found Tina crouched beneath Bella's cage deciding
which bird to target next. She couldn't do much damage be-
yond scaring them, but I worried that if she got too close to
Dusty she'd get her nose nipped through the bars.

Remarkably, our other cats ignored our birds. Frannie
seemed to understand that the birds were under our protection and pretended they didn't exist. Moobie and Lucy
were too fixated on packaged food to look for it on the wing,
Maynard only wanted to be petted, and Agnes spent her
time cultivating grudges. But once Tina discovered our easily spooked parakeets, she became obsessed. She quickly
learned to exploit the weakness of the door that safeguarded
our birds—because technically we didn't have one.

Connecting the front of the house to the kitchen/dining
room where the birds lived was a short passageway that contained the door to the basement. The passageway was so
narrow that when you opened the basement door too far, it
bumped the opposite wall. We had learned to use this design flaw to our advantage by forcing the basement door open
enough that it jammed against the plasterboard and blocked
the passageway.

The system had worked fine, but it was darned inconve-
nient. Closing the basement door could mean three things
in our house. It could mean *closing* the door to close off the
basement, or *opening* the door to close off the bird room. And

it could also mean shutting a completely separate door in the basement that led out to the backyard. Woe unto us if our lives ever depended upon accurately executing the command: *Quick, close the basement door!* We would just stand there and perish.

Tina constantly tested the door to see how firmly it was wedged against the wall. If I had closed off the passageway via a halfhearted shove of the door, a few thumps would open it. If the door was seated too tightly for her to budge, she'd wait for someone to open it and dart through.

We did our best to keep her occupied with other things besides birds. Linda found a dust-covered toy mouse under the dresser, rinsed it off, and tossed it to Tina. She batted it around until it disappeared, then resumed her vigil outside the bird room. I bought another mouse at the store up the street, and it pulled a vanishing act within a few hours, too. Back at the store, I discovered that a sympathetic manufacturer sold fuzzy mice in packs of twelve. "Get that mousie," Linda would cry, breaking one out of the package and heaving it against a wall. After springing for a few more twelve-packs, we learned why our bookcase had started listing to the right. Tina had packed the small space beneath it full of toy mice.

THE ATTENTION THAT we lavished on the new kid wasn't lost on Frannie. She all but abandoned the living room for the basement. In spite of my attempts to shower her with extra attention, she even refused to let me pet her at her feed dish. Outdoors, to pay me back she doubled down on her bird hunting, forcing me to set up another loop of fencing in order to save the birdbath from being a bull's-eye.

One afternoon she alarmed me by tussling with a squirrel beneath the pine tree. Mr. Nutkin emerged unharmed from the opposite side, leaped to the top of the pump house, and shimmied up the hackberry tree. Frannie lingered under the boughs. Before dark she limped inside and hid behind the bed.

"Is your leg okay?" I asked her. My solicitations had the predictable result of urging her to hobble deeper into the shadows.

The next morning, Agnes, Moobie, Lucy, Maynard, and Tina each received a dollop of canned cat food, while I spoiled Frannie with a minced portion of the greasiest chicken dark meat I could find. She wouldn't even raise her chin to glance at it. Later she limped past the food to use the porch litter box, ignored my enthusiastic praises as she bobbled by me, and concealed herself back behind the headboard. Lucy tried to reach Frannie's chicken, but Tina scrabbled over her and scarfed up the food. A suddenly animated Frannie rose up on all fours and hissed.

"She seems to be in a lot of pain," I said. "I'd better take her to the vet."

"Give her a day," said Linda. We gave her two. When she

broke the world's record for sleeping in one position without moving, formerly held by Moobie, I made an appointment with Dr. Post. The trick was laying our hands on her since she would only leave the space behind our headboard to nibble at her kibbles or use the litter box in the dead of night. I managed to wiggle between the wall and the side of the bed, but I couldn't reach her. At the other end of the headboard sat a small bookcase. The plan was to sit Linda in its place and have her shoo Frannie in my direction. When I started to twist and slide the bookcase away, Frannie tottered out to the porch. I grabbed the squeaking cat and inserted her into a pet carrier one toenail at a time.

"LET'S PUT HER on the floor and see how she walks," Dr. Post said. To my amazement, Frannie trotted around the examination room without a hint of a limp.

"It was bothering her not even an hour ago," I told her.

She picked her up, set her on the examination table, and felt the leg. "I'm not finding any injury consistent with a squirrel bite," she said. "There's no sign of a break. She could have a soft tissue injury."

"She acts like it's serious."

"How is Frannie getting along with the new one?"

"She's not. Tina's the anti-Frannie. She's playful, fearless, very outgoing, and she seems happy all the time. Frannie is an extremely serious cat."

"And have you been paying a lot of attention to Tina lately?" Frannie sprang down to the floor to emphasize her dislike of any mention of Tina.

"Do you think she's faking an injury to get attention?"

"I've heard of dogs doing that," said Dr. Post. "I haven't seen it in a cat, but you don't want to put it past them. I wouldn't underestimate her ability to get what she wants."

WHILE I WAS picking my jaw up off the floor of Dr. Post's examination room, Linda was balanced on the edge of the bed folding laundry. Most of the load consisted of pathetically tattered washcloths with all of the color beaten out of them after endless hours of birdcage scrubbing and linoleum mopping. Humming a soul-fortifying hymn, Linda had just finished stacking the washcloths into three soft towers rising from the middle of the mattress when Tina bounded up and crashed into them like a child jumping into a pile of autumn leaves.

"That's very naughty," Linda said. But the toppling laundry frightened her and she had already fled the room. Linda tracked her down on the porch. "Did you understand what I said?" The crooked-mouth, wide-eyed stare indicated that the tyke did not and would not take a hint. "People don't need to play with you twenty-four hours a day." To underscore the gravity of the situation, she added, "Here, go get your mousie." When Linda moseyed back into the bedroom to finish the folding, Maynard was sprawled across a divan he had made from the spilled stacks of laundry, looking for all the world like the King of Cat-mandu.

I popped in with Frannie, who ran behind the bed and hid as soon as I opened her carrier. An unchastened and turbo-charged Tina jumped up onto the bed for another round of wrecking ball. Discovering Maynard on top of the rubble, she recognized a comrade in arms and plopped down beside him. Seeing them together brought to mind a favorite saying of Linda's: "What one doesn't think of, the other does." And it didn't take Tina long to come up with another bright idea. She had already stolen the house out from under Frannie's feet. Now it was time to grab the outdoors, too.

THE ONLY CATS that we allowed outside were the ones that had come to us as indoor-outdoor beings. But Tina flew the coop the Saturday after Frannie's vet appointment while I was traipsing back and forth between the goose pen and the basement. She must have been hiding behind the furnace anticipating her escape. I had just finished filling the geese's wading pool and was on my way to shut off the spigot when Tina appeared beneath the bird feeder wearing her usual be-fuddled expression. But she was anything but confused. As I froze and called her name, concerned that she might bolt, she bolted. So I did what any man would do under desperate circumstances. I howled for my wife.

I ran around to the front yard, hit the shoulder of the road, and marched the width of our property searching Linda's gardens for quivering leaves. I hoped that the semitruck that clattered past would send her in the opposite direction even as a cloud of diesel fumes pushed me away from the street. Although the dangers of the woods were less immediate than careening propane trucks, Tina could easily get lost. I had heard of tiny suburban yards that had swallowed pampered house cats whole. They would spend days huddled behind the backyard grille in clear view of the backyard while their owners shouted themselves hoarse.

"I see her!" Linda called. She had spotted Tina's squatty little white-and-caramel-colored body in front of a thicket of weeds. "There's that naughty girl," Linda cried in the most complimentary and inviting tone of voice imaginable. The tip of Tina's periscope tail scanned us for malicious intent, took note of my seething, and disappeared straight into the weeds. In hot and sweaty pursuit I muscled through a wiry barrier of wild black raspberries. The sunlight disappeared as I plunged into an inland sea of ragweed, goldenrod, garlic mustard, and, ironically enough, catnip. Following Linda's sugary warbles through the uncanny darkness, I ran into an impregnable barrier of pokeweed bushes.

Striking my emergency match, I barely missed colliding with the college-age version of myself, who muttered his disgust about the sorry, foolish creature that I and/or he had turned into. Before I could defend myself, Linda called; "I think she's headed for the river." Pawing my way out of the undergrowth, I plodded briskly toward the water, thinking about the coyotes, foxes, raccoons, stray dogs, skunks, owls, nightjars, and chupacabras that would threaten her if she stayed out all night.

After a dozen false sightings, we gave up. "She'll come back when she wants to," Linda said.

"If she can find her way," I said.

Thirty minutes later, while I was buying a bag of crushed oyster shell for the chickens at the First Prize Feed Mill, Linda phoned to tell me that the incident had ended the way these things always ended. Tina showed up scratching at the side door and immediately darted under the dining room table to bother our birds.

Now I could return to fretting about Frannie. The next morning as I searched my bowl of grits for a lump that was small enough to pick up with my spoon, I wondered what I could do to ease her anxiety. And I wondered if Linda had grabbed a box of instant mashed potatoes by mistake until I remembered that my oatmeal often had a similar consistency. "We made a big mistake getting Tina," I said.

"She's doing fine."

"But Frannie isn't," I said. "She's more soured on people now than when we first got her. She does nothing but hide from me now."

"She's just sulking. Do something special for her, and she'll forget all about Tina."

I got a flash of inspiration. "I wonder if cats like grits."

But she showed no sign of budging from her narrow slot between the headboard and the wall no matter what I did. "That Tina isn't anything," I told her. "She's just a normal everyday cat. She isn't someone special like you."

She whacked my hand when I offered her catnip, so I did what I always did when life offered me a challenge. I slid into bed, turned off the lights, and pulled the covers over my head. I once had a friend who had suffered a mental breakdown. Whenever I visited him, I would sit on a chair in one room and he would sit on the floor in the next room with his back against the opposite side of the wall. It felt like that with Frannie. We were two peas in a pod on opposite sides of the headboard. I kept telling her that I loved her as Maynard bounded up onto the mattress and ploughed into my side.

Meanwhile we doubled our efforts to keep Tina out of trouble. Otherwise our potted dragon tree would find itself in the middle of an excavation or the ceramic knickknacks on top of Linda's dresser would acquire the suicidal habits of lemmings.

I grew weary of fishing fuzzy mice out from under the living room bookcase. Linda tried blocking the crack with a towel, but Tina added "dislodge towel" to her to-do list and I ended up having to extract the towel, too. The next time I visited the store up the street, I cruised the pet supplies in search of a toy that would require minimum effort on our part while subjecting Tina to a maximum amount of tiring activity. A laser pointer seemed like just the thing. I couldn't wait to show it to Tina, and she couldn't resist chasing the fiery red dot up and down the walls. But the impossibility of actually catching her prey frustrated her. After a few minutes she whined for her mousie toy.

I wasn't ready to give up on my investment yet. I poked the laser behind the headboard and made restless bug movements on the carpet with the red dot. Thrown, dangled, or rolled objects either intimidated or bored Frannie, depending on their size and proximity. But switching on the laser flooded her with joyful light. Still lying down, she thumped the floor with her forelegs and snapped at the dot with her teeth. When the glowing ladybug proved difficult to grab, she followed it into the living room, sending Maynard and Tina scurrying as she scuffed the rug with her claws chasing the light in ever-tightening circles. Rolling onto her side she continued her spinning pursuit, a break-dancing kitty in the throes of ecstasy.

It turned into a nightly routine. Frannie would seek out my company after dinner, dogging my steps like Maynard and begging me to play like Tina. If Tina was in the living room when I flashed the laser pointer, Frannie would fix me with a face that said *get rid of that thing.*

A few weeks later, Frannie was waiting for me at the door with calculating eyes as I hung my umbrella on our coatrack.

"Sorry, it's too wet," I told her, interpreting her attention as a request to go out. "We're not playing with the bug light right now," I said when she tried to follow me into the dining room. After I tweaked Bella's beak and greeted the other birds, I let her lead me into the bedroom for a nap. As I pulled down the shades and shut the door so that no other cats could horn in, she followed the usual procedure of ducking behind the headboard. After a while, she might venture out for her snooze on the floor beside the bed.

Just as I started to drift off, I felt a thump on the mattress near my feet. I didn't dare move as she paced back and forth before settling down beside me, close but not touching. Her breathing shifted into purring. The extraordinary moment was as satisfying as it was fleeting. Home from the chiropractor, Linda slammed the front door, launching Frannie off the bed like a bullet from a gun. I didn't mind. I couldn't wait to tell Linda what had happened.

I had squishy, squatty little Tina to thank for deepening the bond between Frannie and me via the grasshopper-shaped laser pointer. And the tiny troublemaker had made Maynard happy, too. Since their meeting over a pile of toppled laundry, they had become friends.

Every morning, Maynard would march upstairs so that Linda could get a break from whining, and Tina would follow. Viewed from behind as they climbed the steps, Maynard resembled the fully loaded trailer of a lumber truck while Tina gamboled like a chubby lamb. Once in the room,

Maynard flopped down on the pillow and instantly fell asleep. Tina planted herself near the window to watch birds flittering through the front yard hackberry tree as she dreamed of escaping outdoors. They were our own Ginger and Gilligan marooned on an island where they never quite received the full amount of attention that they craved.

I imagined Maynard in a sailor's cap and Tina in a coconutshell bra brewing plans for rescue as ukuleles chimed in the background. But never in my sitcom-soaked imagination could I possibly have imagined the big change that was about to come over Frannie.

CHAPTER 12

My Brief Career as a Psychic

The friendship between Maynard and Tina thickened. For much of the day, they resembled co-workers in different departments sharing the same shift but bothering us independently according to their individual expertise. Maynard dogged our heels whining for a lap to sit on, while Tina cased the tabletops and shelves for breakable items to drop. When it came to the serious business of snoozing, though, our Gilligan and Ginger teamed up. They slumbered together each morning in the upstairs bedroom during Linda's daily respite from naughty cats. They co-inhabited her study overnight, side by side on a pair of crocheted beds on top of her desk. And each afternoon when I toppled over for a nap flat on my back, while Maynard butted my ribs and threw himself down at my side, Tina delicately arranged herself around the uncomfortable crevice between my ankles. Linda called it Tina's tuna boat. If Tina tarried in the living room as the rest of us gathered on the bed, Linda would warn her, "You'd better get in here or the tuna boat's going to leave without you."

Frannie didn't even make it to the gangplank. She would never consider setting sail for the Land of Nod or chasing a glowing ladybug across the rug if another cat's presence sullied the room. Linda clomping down the hallway might send her racing to the door squeaking to go out onto the porch, which she considered to be her private domain and the next best thing to being outside. Despite her moments of ease with me, she was only visiting and had her bags packed and heaped upon the front sidewalk anticipating her imminent departure. I wished I could discover what her life had been like before she came to us, so I could understand her case of the jitters.

Linda vowed that she'd try to find out. Innocent souls living up and down the road from us—blameless folks who minded their own business and didn't bother anybody else—received at least one phone call from my wife asking if they knew anything about Frannie. She even placed a classified ad in the local weekly newspaper seeking information about "a white-and-black cat we've had for over a year," and it sounded so much like a coded message that I resigned myself to foreign intelligence agents tapping our phone. But white-and-black cats were apparently as rare as four-leaf clovers, though nowhere near as lucky, and we never received a single response except for vans with tinted windows parking in front of our house at night.

When it came to exercising patience, I was less like the sparrow that scrapes its beak against a mountain once a day until the mountain eventually wears down to the size of a pebble and more like a two-minute egg. The animals that I loved the most were the most skilled at pushing my buttons. Dusty could be banging the bars of his cage at mealtime, sending Linda into paroxysms, and I wouldn't notice. But if Bella merely paced back and forth a few times on her perch, I would shoot up from my chair and tell her, "I just fed you." I was so tuned into my parrot that her whispers came across as shouts. I felt the same way with Frannie.

As I fretted about how unfathomable our pets were, I trudged into the bedroom and discovered Maynard kneading Linda's discarded sweater, face buried in a fold as if suckling from his mother. At that moment I realized that certain aspects of our cats would remain a mystery.

I WAS READING a book about life on a farm and marveled at how well the author knew her animals. *The Long Road Home* was a true story about a group of horses that Kathleen Schurman had rescued, but she told the tale from the point of the nonhuman residents of her Locket's Meadow Farm. I generally didn't enjoy the anthropomorphism shtick, because I felt it reduced the complexity of critters. This time the personalities rang true, from wild crows to spoiled pet ducks and parrots, and I wished I could learn the author's observational skills and deal more successfully with our unruly misfits.

I located Kathleen on the Web and shot her an e-mail telling her how much I enjoyed the book, never expecting to hear back from anyone as important as an author. But she took time out from caring for genuine farm animals—not just the poultry we puttered around with—and told me that she wrote *The Long Road Home* by sitting quietly in the yard and listening to what the animals were saying. I took this as metaphor at first. But a couple of e-mails later she made it clear that she could actually tune into their thoughts and feelings—and that anyone could do the same thing with a little practice.

Although I happily entertained lots of far-flung ideas—I'd encountered feline ghosts, and I believed that extraterrestrials probably abducted me but threw me back as way too weird—I couldn't wrap my head around the idea of animal communication. My thoughts constantly lied to me about who I was and about the world around me depending on how tired, nervous, angry, or foolish I happened to be at a particular moment, and I imagined that most people suffered from a similar insanity. So why trust a mental message allegedly from a hen or duck? It sounded even more far-fetched when Kathleen said that she could receive impressions from a pet just by looking at its photograph. But when she offered to do this with a photo of Frannie, I not only immediately suspended my disbelief; I also put it into a trance and sent her the photo.

Kathleen wrote back the next day. She felt that Frannie was "very sensitive, possibly with a touch of kitty PTSD" despite the fact that the photo I had sent her showed what appeared to be a calm and in-charge cat lounging in the grass. Then she asked, "Do you have an orange-and-white short-haired cat? She's showing me one, but I don't know where it's from." I nearly fell off my swivel chair. When I replied that this had to be Tina, she said, "I got the feeling Frannie felt she was a thorn in her side. She does say she accepts the other cat, but she isn't exactly thrilled with her."

According to Kathleen, before coming to us, Frannie had lived in a trailer or first-floor apartment: "But I don't feel she was in the house much. There was a woman who paid attention to her, and then she was gone. Frannie doesn't know what happened. She just went away. The people that remained were very sad and functioning on a very low level. She shows me a middle-aged man, kind of heavy, dark hair, no smiles at all. They kept feeding her, but no one gave her any affection. And then they just faded away, at least to her mind, and there was no reason to stay. It's the sadness that so affected her. It just cuts to her core. She may not have come directly to you, there may have been a few places where she was fed along the way, but nothing felt right to her."

The account felt right to me and made me feel more

fortunate than ever that Frannie had managed to find us. Whether or not it reported the gospel truth about her origins, the major shadings seemed consistent with her personality and behavior. I liked the fact that it gave me a story where there had only been a void.

Linda was skeptical when I shared Kathleen's e-mail. "It's interesting, but I don't know about her being able to read Frannie's thoughts."

"Then how do you explain her knowing about Tina?"

"I think she's probably reading *your* mind," she told me, as if that were the most normal thing in the world.

Thinking about it later, I decided that both of us were wrong. Frannie was the psychic one. She knew that someone in the world would love her, and she had found me like an arrow finds a bow.

KATHLEEN INSISTED THAT anyone could do it. The difficult part was shutting off the roaring noise of my thoughts and opening myself to faint impressions from Frannie. The easy part was relaxing, though my expertise in this area turned my experiments into naps. I tried choosing a time of day when I didn't sag with weariness, but such a time of day didn't exist. One afternoon after waking from a snooze I seemed to be having some success. I received an image of Frannie trotting down a railroad track, and while I realized that I had simply conjured up a cliché of the vagabond life, I stayed with it until Frannie's path was barricaded by a moose tonguing a salt block. In the finest tradition of Moobie's slurping grooming sessions, Maynard had interrupted my reverie by licking himself.

After another interruption, I lost both Frannie and the moose. I shooed Maynard off the bed, but he didn't disappear completely. If our cats weren't in the room with us, we had to guess where they might be—except for Maynard, who advertised his whereabouts via self-pitying yowls worthy of a child caught in a heating duct. I had never met another cat who would remove himself to the most distant corner of the house and then complain about his removal. This time he had managed to push his way through the basement door and was bawling from the bottom of the stairs about the raw deal that fate had awarded him.

He refused to move a muscle when I dragged myself out of bed to call him, except to unhinge his jaw and protest more loudly. He let me chase him around the staircase a few dozen times before turning into a concrete block and cementing himself to the floor. Normally I would have let him stay in the basement, but I knew without having to read his mind that he intended to lurk until I opened the door to cajole Frannie inside, and then he would attempt an escape. I had no choice but to scoop up seventeen pounds of whining cat and carry him up the steps, although my lower vertebrae took exception to the burden.

The next morning the ache in my back barely bothered me, because it had been overwhelmed by layers of hurt radiating from my neck. And I looked as miserable as I felt. My face was breaking out around one side of my mouth. Groping for an answer that would explain both the pimples and the pain, I surmised that the grueling day-in, day-out stress of a part-time job had caught up with me and jangled my nerves.

My diagnosis proved to be accurate insofar as my problem involved nerves. An inflammation caused by the varicella-zoster virus, which had lazed around in my nerve endings since a childhood bout of chicken pox, had belatedly come out to play and the name of the game was shingles. I was officially a senior citizen now with or without a restaurant discount punch card. Within three days, I resembled a Bat-man villain. Stinging blisters covered the left side of my face, while the right side remained as clear as a baby's elbow, if the baby happened to be a man in his late fifties. But I wasn't able to launch a crime spree that would bring Gotham City to its knees.

"It feels like there's an iron helmet on my head, and every ninety seconds somebody whacks the helmet in a different spot with a hammer," I blubbered to my family physician, Dr. Bhattacharya. She gave me meds to slow the virus and pain-killers to help me sleep. Little did I know that illness could be an aspiring psychic's invisible friend.

Prescription analgesics and I didn't get along. I couldn't even take some over-the-counter pills without end-ing up under the counter. But slabs of pain sent me hurtling to my bottle of Vicodin. I wolfed down two or three—who was counting?—and dumped my sorry self into the upstairs bed to spare Linda a night of seismic mattress shocks as I flinched, shuddered, and groaned. After a while the ouchies continued on unabated, but I experienced them from the opposite side of a cottony wall. Gradually my body melted into the sheets and my untethered brain began to gravitate toward Frannie.

I tried one of Kathleen's animal communication exercises. This time the weak video images of a cat on the tracks stayed behind at the station. Instead, thanks to a sense-numbing combination of illness, exhaustion, and modern medicine, a freight train weighted down with absurdly specific imagery scooped me up. It kept playing and replaying for the next hour or so despite my waking up and falling back asleep. I could barely tell the difference between the two states until I finally snapped on the light and started writing down everything that I could remember.

I prepared to toil through the night describing the epic that had unreeled in front of my closed eyes. Ten minutes and a single steno-size notebook page later, I had reached the end of my need for ink. There wasn't much *there* there. I had mistaken intensity for immensity, but the scenes had been so vivid that the backyard with wildly overgrown bushes where Frannie used to live still pulsated around me.

I had seen the low-pitched roofline of a one-story house with ornamental scalloping around the eaves and windows.

A man in his sixties slumped into the yard carrying a basket and wearing a lightweight dark blue jacket with a high school insignia over the pocket. His glumness was so profound that if the sun had been shining, he would have blotted it out. I felt the presence of the river behind him through the trees. When I saw him next he was inside the house slouched upon a recliner against a wood-paneled wall. He still wore the school jacket. He wore it everywhere and called himself "the coach," but I didn't get the impression that anyone else used the term.

I heard him mutter the word *Charlene,* which was either Frannie's name or referred to a thirty-one-year-old woman in a white sweater standing in a pile of autumn leaves where the man had dropped the basket. She was an attorney working for a Realtor, and her boss had just transferred her to another city. Although she considered the relocation to be an opportunity for advancement, she was bitter because her manager had relocated her out of spite. She didn't like leaving Frannie behind, but I didn't sense a strong connection between them. Both she and the older man seemed emotionally empty with eyes focused on the past. She was tall, thin, and plain faced with short dark hair in a kind of bubble cut.

I applauded myself for the level of detail I had unearthed until I realized that it couldn't have come from Frannie. What would a cat know about office politics or a man who still thought of himself as a high school coach? I had just finished reading John Updike's *Rabbit Run* and the only nonhuman mind I had succeeded in probing was undoubtedly my own.

Popping a sleeping pill, I called it quits for the night and resolved to try again.

No LIVING PERSON had a more defeatist attitude toward being sick than I did. In the throes of the vilest flu,
Linda wouldn't miss a beat of her animal chores. "If I'm going
to feel bad anyway, I might as well be doing something," she
would say. That sort of logic sailed out the window whenever
I had a scratchy throat and lay stock still in bed waiting for
death to flutter down. A more serious illness like shingles
required an extra injection of pessimism. I heaped guilt on
top of the physical discomfort, blaming myself for having
stirred up the virus in the first place. I hadn't been eating
right. Or negative thinking was to blame. God was punish-
ing me for getting crabby with Linda. Or maybe my immune
system had completely collapsed. With all these cheery no-
tions buzzing around inside my head, it was little wonder I
couldn't tune into Frannie. My mental radio was plagued by
constant static.

I phoned Bill Holm to tell him that I wouldn't be available
for dinner at the Chinese buffet that week. "Unless I wore a
burka, I'd clear the place." I described the blisters on my face
and carped about how I had to keep a washcloth soaked in
a bowl of ice water next to the bed. "The itching wakes me
up at night and I can't stand it. I scratch my face and make
it worse."

"Do you still have Moobie's Elizabethan collar?"

"Not that again," I told him. "You'd have a bad attitude, too, if you felt like this."

"It has nothing to do with attitude. You need to wear her cone to keep from scratching yourself." The idea delighted him. "You've got to do it!"

A lightning bolt shot through my ear on its way to fry my molar, and I used the pain as an excuse to hang up. Bill was right, of course—right about what he didn't actually say and didn't even intend to imply, but which I attributed to him based on my principles of self-reproach. I should emulate Frannie, Moobie, Agnes, Lucy, Tina, and Maynard—well, okay, not Maynard—and take events as they came. I needed to roll with the punches, but the taps from life's index finger knocked me flat before I had the chance. Fortunately for me, psychological relief soon arrived. Unfortunately, it came out of a bottle.

Dr. Bhattacharya had prescribed a popular corticosteroid tablet to help relieve the pain and prevent long-term nerve damage from my shingles. The steroid had a wonderful side effect. In addition to giving me super strength, which I could take or leave because I wasn't any less lazy than before, the pharmaceutical improved my frame of mind. It somehow located the "mute" button inside my skull and by thirty or so decibels toned down the endless stream of internal chatter that second-guessed every move I made no matter how infinitesimally inconsequential. Free from obsessive mental noise at last, I was no longer congenitally alienated from my surroundings. I had ceased to be "the coach" in the nylon high school jacket.

I shared my good news with Linda. "This must be what it feels like to be a normal person," I told her. I couldn't wait to crawl into bed that night and attempt a Vulcan mind meld with Frannie. I smelled a psychic breakthrough.

I DECIDED NOT to add Vicodin to my overnight cocktail, saving it for a special treat in case I awoke in headthrobbing misery in the wee hours of the morning. I thought about Frannie after snapping off the light. She had been more attentive lately, rubbing against my leg and fixing me with her ferret-faced stare as I sat reading a Bill Bryson book in the living room. So as I located my comfortable spot in the bed, I tried connecting with her past and tuning into something other than an episode of *Charlene and the Coach*. Instead I received an image of her trotting up to me as I took my afternoon nap, hopping onto my chest, and curling up for a snooze.

I rated this scene as even less believable than the previous flashbacks. Although she had graduated from her apprenticeship on the bedroom floor, whenever she joined me at mattress level she always kept her distance. The thing she hated most in life was being picked up, and she had never climbed up on my lap or so much as draped a paw across my ankle. Even petting her with two hands was taboo.

Having struck out at Kathleen's communication exercise, I

paged through my field guide to birds and tried to learn the sparrows until my sleeping pill kicked in. When I turned on the light, I was shocked to discover Frannie camped out in the doorway to my room. She never slept upstairs and went out of her way to avoid tussling with the other cats. Agnes had parked herself on my desk chair pretending that nothing extraordinary had taken place. But it had. I experienced a non-shingles-related tingling as I realized that Frannie was worried about me. She was showing me the same devotion that we had shown her after her accident. Although I might have expected this kind of loyalty from a dog, I never imagined that a cat would be motivated by concern for me.

She still hadn't stirred from her post a few hours later when I got up to gulp down some water. I needed to refill my glass for next time but I'd inadvertently emptied the doorway as I headed out of the bedroom; I had lurched forward too quickly, startling Frannie and sending her fleeing downstairs into the gloom. Later, though, a soft form rubbing against my side awakened me. I barely moved, not wanting to scare her. My arms were already raised to keep the covers from rubbing up against my face, so I slowly turned one wrist toward the cat. I pressed the stem of my watch with my other hand to plunge the room into a faint green light. The cat whose eyes shone back at me was Agnes. Since I had moved upstairs, she couldn't get enough petting.

I directed the watch-light toward the doorway. Frannie was nowhere to be seen.

I HAULED MYSELF out of bed the following morning feeling miserable and sorry for myself. I had missed an entire week of work, and although lying around all day should have been a dream come true, the bed rest was tiring me out and making me even crabbier than usual. The previous night's exhilaration over Frannie's concern for me had dried up. The way I saw it, she offered me devotion without a lot of trust to back it up. All it took to shake her faithfulness was a footstep in her direction. She was in love with the idea of love but skedaddled from its clunky reality.

When I groused to Linda about my interrupted night and added that my shingles didn't seem to be getting any better, she tilted my face toward the window, and pronounced a definite improvement. "I'm going to end up with all kinds of scars," I told her. "I'll go through life looking like an asteroid."

"I thought you said your steroid had given you a positive outlook."

"She cancelled it out," I said, pointing to Tina. My current mood didn't welcome the antics of an overgrown kitten. Linda had discovered that the orange-and-white cat was shredding a section of the bathroom wallpaper, and her handiwork appealed so much to Frannie, that she had started using the spot as her scratching post, too. As I sat on the edge of the bed searching for an AM radio station that wasn't spewing out political talk, Tina shot into the room using vertical surfaces as her horizontal raceway and never touching foot to floor.

She mistook me for a playmate. Linda had given Tina a

taste of the squid I'd purchased long ago for Lucy, and now she craved it all day long. She glared at me with double search-lights, using not-so-psychic communication techniques as I fiddled with my radio. Unable to locate anything worth lis-tening to, I set the Grundig back on top of Linda's dresser and made the mistake of resting my hand on the front of the top drawer in which "squiddy" lived. Tina pogoed up to meet my fingers and connected claw with flesh.

Kicking the door shut as I booted her out, I tuned in a Con-temporary Hit Radio station that I loathed and turned up the volume to sustain my bad mood. As I slid under the covers and revved up for a hearty session of feeling sorry for myself, Frannie tiptoed out from behind the headboard. She didn't hesitate. She skipped up to the mattress, climbed onto my chest, and eased herself down on my ribs as if she had been planning to do this for days.

Had she put this image in my mind, or had she gotten the idea from me? I lifted an arm and started to pet her. As she began to purr and as her body radiated warmth into mine, I felt just then that my illness had begun to loosen its hold. In some sense Frannie was making me aware of the healing pro-cess just as I had been helping her to heal herself from what-ever had happened to her in the past. Our mutual anxiety melted away. She didn't flinch when I raised my other arm to stroke her with both hands at once. Our relaxation deepened as Lady Gaga gained intensity in the background. My fingers knitted together over her spine. Ever so gently I pressed her against me.

I murmured just one word. I said, "Charlene."

LATER IN THE day I e-mailed Kathleen to tell her what had happened. I was so excited that I peppered my message with more than the usual helping of misspellings and deleted words. "Keep trying with Frannie. I think she wants you to know her story from the very beginning," Kathleen wrote. "I'm getting some previous connection between the two of you, but I don't know what it is. She certainly went to a lot of trouble to find you."

I thought I'd test my talents with another member of the house. Bella had bitten my sister Bett when she visited us from Indiana recently. I had been rubbing the parrot's neck by sticking my finger through the bars and invited my sister to do the same. "She absolutely, positively, one hundred percent will not bite you," I assured her. The next thing I knew, Bett was blotting her bloody finger on a paper towel.

I knew Bella's history and simply wanted to get inside her head. And so I sat with her, waiting to hear her story. But Bella just stared back at me. Instead I drifted back to Frannie and suddenly understood how she felt inside the house. Whenever I approached her wanting to pet her—and even just talking to her at times—I was emanating these waves of human energy at her. I could almost see a series of

ripples shooting from my hands as if I were Mandrake the
Magician casting a spell, and I understood why she retreated
into the basement.

The next morning I awoke encased in a deeper level of
calm than I had experienced in years. I felt connected to our
birds as I diced up their fruit. Out in the barn I suddenly
understood that if I moved too quickly among the ducks and
hens, they interpreted my haste as pursuit or flight. Either
made them nervous, so I resolved to slow down.

"Thanks so much for teaching me these animal communication techniques," I told Kathleen. "It's making a huge
change in my life."

BUT MY BRIEF career as a psychic soon came to a
screeching halt, if it had ever actually existed. Over the next
few days I began to wonder if the whole thing hadn't been a
hallucination brought on by prescription drugs and a level
of boredom verging on sensory deprivation. Once I returned
to my job, popped my final corticosteroid tablet, and sub-
sequently got gonged by an uptick in shingles pain, my astral
body turned back into a homebody that said phooey to stray-
ing from my frame. That old familiar gang of mental noise,
impatience, and darting movements had revisited and re-
trenched. When I lay in the dark upstairs and tried to let my
mind drift purposefully toward Frannie, I started obsessing
instead about the drab brown warbler I had seen in our pine

tree and combed through the twists and turns of my brain to identify it.

Yet Frannie and I had suddenly become more finely attuned to each other, as if we were both monitoring the same CB channel. I instantly understood the glance from her that said, "I'll eat that canned cat food product if you stop presenting it to me on a china saucer and put it in my bowl where it belongs." For her part, although she didn't take a snooze on my bony chest again, she would plop down beside me with her front paws curled over my arm—as long as there were no other cats in the room.

In the long run, I didn't feel overly deprived by not being able to hear the voices of animals the way that Kathleen could. I realized that every pet owner was already essentially a mind reader. You had to be one to keep up with your critters. And anyway, the occasional psychic blip still kept me going.

Not long after my psychic phase, Claire, a Facebook friend from South Africa, shared the sad news that her elderly cat, Coco, had passed away. She sent me a photo of the cat. I found myself e-mailing her. "I have a weird question to ask about Coco," I wrote. "Do you have a patio with potted plants where Coco liked to sleep? I just had an impression of that while studying her picture. I felt a lot of leafy green around her. Also, was there something with her and a wooden gate, maybe in the front yard?" Coco's photo had given me an itch that I couldn't stop myself from scratching.

I was shocked when she replied, "You are amazingly accurate in your intuition. Coco enjoyed a balcony with potted plants where she would sunbathe. Also you asked about a wooden gate. When we lived in Durban we were in an old Cape Dutch house that had a wooden front door like you might find on a stable. When Coco went out at night she would come back at some ungodly hour and knock on the bottom of the door with her paw. The door, being a little loose, would make a hell of a bang!"

Claire wondered how I had known about the potted plants and the old rustic door. To my mind the critical question wasn't *how?* but *why?* With six cats crowded under one small roof, why was I poking my nose into the afterlife of a seventh kitty on the other side of the globe?

I should have pointed my eyeballs at a group photo of our gang and tried to intuit what was to come. But it would have taken Carnac the Magnificent to predict the sudden added complexity that lurked just around the corner.

. . . .

CHAPTER 13

Living in a Walled City

W hy is Tina's chin so dirty all the time?"
Linda asked.

This didn't seem like a question that would end up plunging us into so much chaos that I'd forget about my obsession with Frannie. It wasn't as if Linda had asked me, "Did I mention that I bought a pair of emus yesterday?" Or "Say, have you happened to notice the termite swarm in the living room?" She had simply called attention to the apparent lack of cleanliness of Tina's chin, though it would turn out to be horrendously more complicated than that.

Although it didn't seem connected to Tina's chin, we also had an ongoing problem with our kitchen door that wasn't a kitchen door. When we jammed open the basement door to seal off the passageway, any cat in the basement could race up the stairs and end up shut inside with our parakeets, parrots, doves, and rabbits. Keeping track of the cats was easy when we had two or three. But now, six meant that we often slipped up and encountered Tina, Maynard, Lucy, or even Agnes wandering around in the bird room.

I thought that we had solved the door dilemma with a product called the SeeNoScreen, but the solution depended to a large extent upon an illusion. Designed for outside doors, the SeeNoScreen pulled down in window-shade fashion from a spring-loaded ceiling-mounted roll. The jaunty gray-and-white-striped transparent appearance made me feel like I was stepping into a beach cabana whenever I raised the screen and passed from living room to kitchen. Although the bottom of the screen latched to the floor, the sides hung in space flapping against the passageway walls. Fortunately the tightly stretched mesh appeared solid enough that our cats treated the insubstantial material as if it were made of brick.

It even fooled Tina, whose desire to make a plaything out of anything should have revealed the secret of the permeable barrier. My sister Joan watched in amazement as I pulled down the screen to prevent Tina from joining us in the dining room. I plucked Bella out of her cage, plunked her down on the countertop, and repeatedly handed her a paper cup, which she repeatedly tossed to the floor. Tina whined on the other side of the screen.

"I can't believe that thing works," Joan said. "Our cats would walk right through it. Or they'd shred it first."

I tut-tutted about the naughtiness of Joan's kitties. But the damage had already been done. Tina had overheard her.

"WHAT'S THAT SORE on your chin?" Linda asked Tina. "It doesn't look like dirt. It looks like acne. How can a cat get acne?"

Drawn to bad information on the Web like a graham cracker to staleness, I convinced myself that Tina had a feline version of the common skin disorder seborrhea. Following the advice from my online source, I bought a bottle of anti-dandruff scalp medication and rubbed it into Tina's chin. It smelled like facial cleanser I had used in my pimply past and it triggered a wave of nostalgia that sent me spinning back to my high school days—and to my college days, graduate school days, and fifty-fifth birthday. The stuff didn't work any better on Tina than it had worked on me. A few days later when we found an ugly bump on her gums, I raced her to the vet.

Dr. Post told me that she probably had a food allergy "Some cats develop a sensitivity to specific proteins, or they're allergic to dyes and additives."

"The very things that make life worth living."

"Well, I don't think she'll miss those as much as you might if we switch her to a limited-ingredient diet," she said. "Something that doesn't contain chicken, beef, or seafood."

When Dr. Post told me which particular animal protein

Tina's food would include, I changed the subject. "I read on-line that cats usually grow out of food allergies," I said.

"They usually don't. She'll have to stay on a special diet for the rest of her life."

At the front desk I picked up the antibiotic to treat the abscess in Tina's mouth and filled out loan papers for a few ounces of her special kibbles. But I wasn't thinking about the cost as I pulled into the driveway. Another matter weighed upon my mind.

Just before dinner, I strolled out to close up the barn and was delighted to discover a dead mouse near one of the feed bins. Our Muscovy duck Victor didn't suffer from any aller-gies. His fondness for rodent protein had shocked me the first time that I saw him eat a mouse, but now I indulged him whenever I had the chance. I picked up lifeless Mickey by the tail and flipped him toward our Donald. The ex-mouse barely struck the floor before Victor recognized him as a delicacy. He snatched him in his beak, threw back his head, swal-lowed, and panted with pleasure, wagging his massive tail in celebration.

"Sorry, buddy," I told Victor before I clicked off the lights. "We just have to chalk up the matter as part of the big circle of life." I wasn't talking about the mouse.

Some people called me the duck man. Some people called me the gangster of love—mistakenly so, in my opinion. But loving ducks is what I was known for. So as I trudged back into the house and was met by a searchlight-eyed Tina on the porch, I was nagged by guilt as I heaped green-pea-and-duck-formula kibbles into her dish.

DUCKS AROUND THE world quacked in celebration when I decided that we could only afford to feed Tina the kibbled gold even though our other cats would have benefited from the healthy ingredients. All that I needed to do was shut her inside Linda's study at mealtime. What could be easier!

Except that our kitties didn't have a mealtime hour. We filled their bowls and let them graze as their stomachs moved them, and I knew they wouldn't like conforming to a schedule. Once we started moving their dishes out of Tina's reach, Lucy engaged in retaliatory litter box overshoots and increased biting. Agnes showed up downstairs to hiss at the other cats. Maynard wailed more than ever. Only Moobie showed no reaction to the change, because nothing much changed for her. In deference to her age and decrepitude, I fed her a dollop of meat and meat by-product whenever I found her camped alongside the SeeNoScreen, which interrupted her pilgrimage to the refrigerator.

I hadn't realized how many food dishes were scattered throughout the house until I had to raise and lower them at feeding time. Lucy had a dish in the front hallway. Maynard and Tina each had one in Linda's study. Frannie had one on the front porch and another in the basement for nights on mouse patrol. Agnes somehow ended up with a pair in different rooms upstairs. And Moobie's dish might be anywhere.

It followed her around, at the ready whenever she was willing to eat, and it even had its own zip code. Remembering to collect all of the dishes after the cats had finished eating wasn't easy considering that my brain was already overloaded with details of caring for our fifty-some animals. I didn't need yet another problem, but Frannie gave me one.

I walked into the bathroom to find her standing on her hind legs vigorously scratching the wallpaper. While she and Tina had done minor damage to it before, this looked as if we had leased our wall to a gypsum strip-mining company.

"Frannie's going to find herself living outdoors," I told Linda.

"You wouldn't like that," Linda said. But from the look on her face I could tell that she was warming to the idea.

"She shouldn't still be acting like the wild woman of Borneo," I said. "She should be a lot more domesticated by now."

"She's hardly wild. She's the most pampered cat in the house. And Tina does it, too, blast her little hide."

Linda called our handyman, Gary, who recommended covering the bottom twenty-six inches of the wall with a thin sheet of bead board. "I can paint it white and add a piece of trim along the top. It'll look nice and clean and they won't be so tempted to claw it."

But I calculated that it would be cheaper simply to keep the bathroom door closed twenty-four hours a day. Instead, I spent way too much money on a pneumatic door-closing device. "Give me a call if anything comes loose," Gary told me after he had installed it, conveying his doubts about its effectiveness. The closed door opened stiffly now.

"Sorry," I said as I pushed on the door and the pneumatic cylinder pushed back. "I didn't think anyone was in here."

"Are you talking to me?" Linda asked from down the hall.

Once local wallpaperer Wilma re-wallpapered our wall, the bathroom problem seemed to have been solved every bit as neatly as our kitchen door problem—meaning neither of them had actually been solved at all.

MY PSYCHIC RAPPORT with Frannie had long since faded and I hadn't made any further breakthroughs. Instead of tuning into me she was fixated on competing with Tina.

One afternoon I found her parked in front of the closed door as Tina crunched on her special kibbles inside Linda's study. Frannie wanted some of that food. She told me so with the same clarity you would use when communicating with a child. She led me from my upstairs office to the porch, posed at her dish with a well-practiced expression of expectancy, then danced over to rub her cheek against the bag of Tina's kibbles.

"Do you want some 'duck food'?" I asked. Tina hadn't taken to the taste of her pricey food at first, and when I slipped up once and presented a bowl of it to Maynard, he walked off in disgust. But Frannie meowed delightedly as I sprinkled it on top of her cat chow like a garnish. She attacked her food with gusto. I decided to take advantage of her elevated mood and pet her with both hands. She hadn't let me do that since she had taken a nap on my chest while I had shingles. But the trust just wasn't there. She squeaked and bolted.

The next morning, she raced up from the basement and stared at a saucer of greasy chicken. I normally didn't let her inside the kitchen/dining room with the birds but made an exception for her breakfast treat when I was in the room. Tina stared longingly at the snack from the other side of the SeeNoScreen. Just to taunt her, Frannie left the chicken untouched and scampered back down the basement stairs. I followed to look for a dish towel. When I returned I found Tina in the kitchen licking the saucer clean. She had finally pieced together Joan's comments about the SeeNoScreen design and broken into the kitchen.

Her triumph didn't take me completely by surprise. Over time the condition of our once proud screen had eroded. It no longer resembled a formidable metallic force field but instead a remnant from the shattered window of a prospector's shack. The manufacturer had designed the SeeNoScreen to withstand being raised and lowered a few times a day as opposed to every seventy seconds. The constant use had aged it quickly. And the engineers hadn't constructed the screen according to Linda-proof specs—if such standards of indestructibility were even possible. In spite of her small stature, my wife effortlessly snapped vacuum cleaner handles like twigs, tore the glove compartment out of one of her cars, and wore down shoes while sitting still.

She didn't destroy the integrity of so-called durable goods through brute strength alone. She was a walking storage battery for a mysterious subatomic force that pulled manufactured objects backward in time toward a preassembled state of being. Linda's newest pair of glasses started losing screws and popping out lenses the moment she had first set them on her nose.

I'd lived inside Linda's energy field for almost twenty years, and in a turn of cosmic balancing she'd had the opposite effect on me. She had helped me to be as whole as I would ever be.

Dr. Post had told me that it would take six weeks before we'd find out if changing Tina's diet had worked. Her chin started looking better in half that time, and chasing her around the house with a syringe of antibiotics had healed the sore in her mouth. But I still worried about her well-being because I knew a couple of people who would throttle her if she didn't stay out of their bird room.

The secret of the SeeNoScreen's vulnerability spread. Tina had learned to penetrate the barrier by probing it for weaknesses, but Maynard succeeded through head-butting trial and error plus a determination to wail his lamentations from every room of the house. I believed optimistically that I could restore the screen to its former glory through a strategic application of white plastic tape. But mending the bottom and sides didn't impress anyone except me. I admitted surrender the morning that I raised the SeeNoScreen to find Moobie waiting for me by the refrigerator. The screen now only succeeded in impeding our movement, while providing an effortless portal for the cats.

Once again Gary came to our rescue.

Although Linda didn't use the Internet, she wielded the telephone with a humbling level of mastery. She sweetly bludgeoned the most uncooperative hardware-store clerks into describing in molecular detail any types of divider doors on their premises. One man admitted that he had what Linda was looking for and then spontaneously confessed to having once glimpsed a white-and-black cat in his front yard. Having extracted the maximum amount of information from this now broken individual, she dispatched Gary to pick up a two-panel folding door in his truck.

Linda ordered the door at the correct height for our space and as close to the right width as she could find for a one-hundred-year-old house that resisted conforming to building codes. As Gary measured and re-measured the doorway he realized that the only thing square about the angles was the Calvinist farmer who had built them in 1907. Not only was there a full quarter-of-an-inch difference in width between the top and bottom of the doorway, but also enough variation in the height to make the most unflappable track-style folding door literally lose its groove.

The door required so much reconstruction that Gary had to insert metal rods into the two top frames to keep it from falling apart. To us, it was a thing of beauty, though—made all the more attractive by the vanquished slump of Tina's body when she discovered she could no longer slip on through.

With a solid door where none had been before, the house felt more closed in than ever. Tina chomped her kibbles locked in Linda's study, and the wheezing pneumatic cylinder kept the bathroom door shut. Disliking confinement with people or cats, Frannie sought seclusion on the porch and grew dissatisfied with the mere sprinkling of Tina's chow on top of hers. "You want your 'duck food,' Frannie?" I asked as I added a handful to her bowl. When I shut the porch door behind me, I found Linda standing in the middle of the living room with her arms crossed.

"It's like living in a walled city," she said. "It's too claustrophobic. Can't we at least keep the bathroom door open?"

So we called Gary back to follow his original plan of covering the bottom twenty-six inches of the wall with a thin sheet of bead board. He painted it white and added a piece of trim along the top. "It looks okay," he said when he had finished. "It looks clean." And I was still so elated over our folding door that paying for two bathroom anti-cat measures didn't bother me. The sitcom of my life boiled down to a series of reruns, though I didn't yet realize that we had just entered a season of endless repeats.

"WE WERE DOING fine for a while. But now we keep forgetting to put all the bowls away and Tina manages to find one," I told Joan. She had twelve cats now, including one with a food allergy. "How do you keep Winston out of everybody else's bowl?"

"We don't. We feed all of them the same food."

I tried to find out as diplomatically as possible if Jack had discovered a uranium deposit behind the garage. But it turned out that he hadn't fallen into a glowing pit of cash. Joan told me that a local pet supplies megastore boasted oodles of limited-ingredient diets at half the cost of the kibbles I was buying from my vet. I went online and printed out the particulars of a green-pea-and-duck-formula food that the store carried and ran it by Dr. Post, who said that she couldn't find anything wrong with it. I should have checked with the cats, too. It looked at first like they would rather starve than allow me to save a cent. But once Frannie noticed Tina sniffing the stuff, she decided that she had to have whatever interested her nemesis.

Even though all of the cats were now eating the specialty kibbles, Frannie still insisted that I go through the motions of sweetening her bowl. "You want some of your 'duck food'?" I asked, and she squeaked as I sprinkled green-pea-and-duck-formula chow on top of her green-pea-and-duck-formula chow. It made her happy, and compared to the cranial calisthenics of keeping several bowls on or off the floor at the appropriate times, this little piece of coddling required minimal energy. But even as Linda and I celebrated the return of mealtime simplicity, Lucy developed bladder complications.

I lugged her up the street to Dr. LeBlanc, who had treated her for a urinary complaint a few years earlier. It had returned with a vengeance. "She has a lot of crystals in her urine, which isn't a good thing," he told me. "But it's a condition that responds well to medication."

"I'd rather give medicine to a crocodile," I told him. "She loves to bite."

"You'll be safe," he said. "You just need to give her a medicated food for six weeks."

That meant we had to go on bowl patrol again to keep one cat out of the other cats' kibbles. "Six weeks?" I said. "That's a month and a half."

"Six weeks for the food that will dissolve the crystals. After that, she'll need to be on a special maintenance diet for the rest of her life."

The phrase "the rest of her life" struck a nerve. I had never thought of Lucy as anything but a permanent nuisance. Back at home I heard myself telling her, "You'll feel better soon, sweetie," as I tried to pet her without getting nipped. Having to like her in addition to loving her struck me as an unfair burden.

WITH A SICKENING sense of déjà vu, we returned to the mealtime regimen that we thought we had sloughed off. The cats weren't happy about it, either. They resented the loss of their all-day grazing bounty, but none as much as Lucy. Due to her sedentary nature, I figured that the more far-flung bowls in the house would be safe. But once her frequent litter box visits began to trickle off, I would find her upstairs or in the basement eating out of someone else's dish — or even sprawled across the bench on our front porch with her head lowered into a bag of kibbles.

Our kitchen door solution, our cat barrier, wasn't any more permanent. Among all of our cats, Tina and Maynard were the ones most interested in spending time with us. Maynard craved cuddling, while Tina simply wanted to stare at us. When Linda and I ate dinner on the other side of the folding door, Maynard would complain about it — which made him a lot like me. Tina worked at finding a solution — which made her a lot like Linda.

"Tell me I'm not seeing what I'm seeing," Linda said one night as the door began to shudder. We heard a distinctive meow that was more insistent than plaintive.

"She can't get in here," I said as I shoveled green beans into my mouth.

The door quivered with a purposeful rhythm until a crack emerged and a white-and-carmel-colored face enlarged the gap.

"No chubby little cats allowed," I told her and shooed her out. "That was a fluke," I insisted. "She won't be able to do it again." Within seconds the middle of the door buckled and a pair of owl eyes pierced my tattered optimism.

Tina came and went between the rooms at will until I dug out the baby gate that had done a poor job of keeping Frannie downstairs. We leaned the gate against the folding door.

Now, to go in or out of the dining room, we had to pick up the gate and move it, open the folding door, and then replace the gate behind us. Throughout the day my ears were treated to the sharp crash of the gate hitting the floor as Linda failed to balance it just so. I tried to step over the gate a few times, but after falling over it onto the dining room table, I abandoned the athletic approach.

The bright idea finally struck me of reversing the door so that it no longer pushed open from the living room side.

"Let's see her learn to pull it open," I said a little too smugly.

Linda shook her head. "She's smarter than you think."

For a couple of weeks the dining room fortress held. Then Tina discovered that by doggedly, cattedly banging the leading edge of the door with her paw, the door would pop open just to be rid of her. Even Maynard got into the act and hammered away with his oversize head. Once he had created a yawning passage, in traipsed Moobie, Lucy, Frannie, and a passing herd of elk.

Loathe to reprise our dances with the gate, we racked our brains to devise a latch. I went online and searched out mechanisms for patio doors, trailer doors, cabinet doors, and even shed doors, but they were either too large or couldn't be operated from both sides of the door. But our Gary dabbled in metal sculpture, glass blowing, and other artistic feats. Possessing a genius for thinking outside the box and seeing past the door frame, he made us a nifty bolt that actually slid across the middle of the door to prevent it from folding.

And he capped it with a pair of ornate amber-colored glass knobs for easy operation from both sides. It worked beautifully, though he might as well have used gold nuggets in place of the glass knobs.

After all of the needed renovations and rehangings, we now owned the most expensive two-panel louvered folding door on the planet.

You might think that solving the door problem would have marked the end to our current streak of troubles ushered in by Tina and her dirty chin. You might also think that the Rhine River emptied into Lake Michigan.

"Oh, no, not again," Linda groaned. We were drinking our morning coffee as Maynard hopped up onto the bed. "Look at his chin," she told me. I hung on to him long enough to locate the telltale red bump. "He can't be allergic to the 'duck food,'" Linda said. In addition to Tina's duck-based formula, the pet supplies megastore carried salmon-based, chicken-based, lamb-based, and even venison-based cat kibbles, and I envisioned us trying out limitless limited-ingredient foods until we found one that agreed with all of our non-Lucy cats.

I hauled Maynard to Dr. Post to confirm the diagnosis. Uttering a matter-of-fact "Aha," she announced that Maynard's problem was fleas. "If he doesn't go outdoors, he probably caught them from another cat who does." I thought of Frannie. "You'll have to treat all of them to be sure."

But we hadn't resolved the last of our food issues yet. After playing with the "bug light" in the living room one evening, Frannie led me out onto the porch.

As usual, I took a pinch of the green-pea-and-duck-formula chow from the bag, asked her, "You want some of your 'duck food,' sweetie?" and sprinkled it on top of her green-pea-and-duck-formula chow. But she stared at me instead of eating. I added more and got the same results.

Then it dawned on me what she wanted. I didn't know how I knew, but I knew it with absolute certainty. Trudging across the porch, I unrolled what was left of a bag that hadn't been opened for months, dug out a small handful of food, and dropped it into her dish. "It's your 'duck food,' Frannie," I told her. Accepting my newly expanded definition of the term, she buried her face in her bowl, crunching loudly and arching her back as I petted her.

"Talk about coming full circle," I told Linda when I came back into the house. "Remember when Frannie had to have 'duck food' sprinkled on top of her supermarket cat food? Well, now I'm sprinkling supermarket cat food on top of Frannie's 'duck food.' You just can't win with that cat."

CHAPTER 14

· ·

Funneled Again

I couldn't imagine what Frannie must have been thinking. We had a contract, which I had signed and she had marked with a muddy paw. So it was all very official. She had agreed that she would stay within earshot of the house while she was outdoors, and in return I'd let her decide when she wanted to come back in. She was allowed to get distracted by a praying mantis or sudden activity at a mole's burrow as long as she came running after I called a few times. But clause three stipulated that once she pranced up to the door as I held it open, she was supposed to go through it. She wasn't permitted to veer off in another direction to roll upon the lawn. And when I ambled over to pet her, she was specifically prohibited from pulling her old trick of racing away to taunt me through the boughs of our spruce tree.

Contracts written for cats clearly didn't apply to will-o'-the-wisps, and the usual standards of pet treatment fell by the wayside, too. If Agnes, Moobie, or Lucy had refused to come inside, I would have hauled the cat into the house like a sack of mackerel. But coercing Frannie in any fashion just felt wrong. Ever since her accident, she had developed a phobia about being picked up. If I whisked her up off the ground and carried her inside, it would terrify her for a moment, and even a moment was too long. I also wanted to avoid getting my sternum punctured.

Slogging toward the spot where she was huddling, I faked her out at the last instant by curving past her hidey-hole and putting the barn in my sights. Continuing on behind the poultry pens I followed the gravel path to our neighbor's driveway where Linda used to leave a margarine dish of food for her when she was still a stray. Then I turned around and started searching among the overgrown masses of jewel-weed for catnip plants. I plucked five medium-size leaves that hadn't been turned into lace by leafhoppers, crushed a leaf between my fingers, inhaled the pungent smell, cursed myself for lacking a feline brain, and slipped them all inside my shirt pocket. Getting Frannie high would be risky, since she could just as easily tag my hand with a claw as follow me back to the house. But I didn't have to shoot an herbal arrow after all. She had abandoned the spruce, and to punish me for failing to hang around and wheedle her, she wouldn't show a single hair of her white-and-black head when I called.

I set off a small explosion of activity when I looked for her next to the pump house. A downy woodpecker had been chipping away at a brand new block of suet while a squirrel hung upside down pilfering sunflower seed. They left both feeders swinging when they bolted, taking a pair of mourning doves with them that shot off with clattering wings. Our pet geese trumpeted their dislike of my skulking behavior as I circled the spirea bush in search of the fugitive. Deep in the woods a pewee sang its last song of the day. I thought about following the song to the river, but I didn't suppose that Frannie had wandered that far. A crow agreed with me.

As I shouted from the porch I wondered if our neighbor a quarter of a mile down the street was puzzling over what a "Frannie-sweetie" might be. A tomato red SUV pulled up to our mailbox, executed a U-turn, and left behind a fog of dust as a farewell present. Caught in the cloud, I thought about how the yard would look a few months from now buried in snow. Into such a weird world our Alfalfa gal had appeared a few days after Linda spotted her racing through the woods. Her fragile appearance had surprised me. Since she was eking out a living in the dead of winter, I had expected a fearsome bruiser instead of a wisp of smoke. I remembered that spark of connection when our eyes first met through the bathroom window blinds and I felt protective of her all over again.

I decided what I would do when she came up to the front door again. I'd scoop her up and haul her into the house like a sack of mackerel.

"DID YOU THINK I was calling you?" I asked Moobie.

I was surprised to find a bright-eyed white cat perched on the back of the couch facing the door with the resoluteness of a Foo dog. She spent most of her time sleeping in the closet and rising with the sunset to haunt the bathroom sink, her dish, or a patch of rug in front of the squatty cabinet. She wasn't just winding down in life, she barely had a spring left at all, and I worried about her. As she followed the spine of the couch, her steps were slow and carefully placed. She needed to concentrate to keep her balance. Raising her head to meet my hand, she switched on the purring machine. After I petted her awhile, she plopped down to the floor and slid between Maynard and Tina, who barely noticed the gaunt figure. She trailed me into the bedroom and after one false start managed to hop up onto the mattress. She continued to purr as she arched her back in pleasure.

"You're certainly lovey-dovey today," I told her while she licked my hand. Then I remembered that moments ago I had crushed catnip between my fingers. "Is this what you want?" I floated a leaf down to the bedspread. Torn between eating the nepetalactone delivery device or rolling on it, she did each in turn. When no trace of the leaf remained, she jumped down to the floor, tipped over Linda's wicker wastebasket, and triumphantly flourished a discarded strip of packing tape that I had torn off a parcel of vitamins. Chewing on tape, envelopes, or anything with adhesive had been a quirky pleasure of a younger Moobie, and it buoyed me to watch her transform the tape into a giant Chiclet.

I fished Tina's "squiddy" toy out of Linda's dresser drawer. Closing the bedroom door so that Tina wouldn't horn in on the action, I coaxed Moobie into rolling over on her back and taking kittenesque swipes at the dangling tentacles. As I played with her I realized that the there was a reason that catnip didn't work on people. The herb hadn't caused her joy. It had merely boosted the innate sense of wonder and delight that was central to the nature of every cat. Even sourpuss Lucy was merrily in love with herself and never surrendered a moment of her day to worry. I guessed that if I somehow managed to attain a similar state of continuous contentment, then catnip would pitch me over the railing into a sea of sheer bliss, too.

I thought back to the days after Moobie's surgery when she had been forced to wear the Elizabethan collar. Although the collar had bothered her at first, she ended up transforming it to her advantage. Because I had felt so sorry for her, I treated her to extra helpings of coddling and called the cone her funnel of happiness. But in that sense the collar was redundant. In sickness and in health, and in youth as well as old age, she already wore the funnel of happiness that she had been born with, and she never once took it off.

I figured that I had a funnel of happiness, too. But the problem was that I usually wore it upside down, and the joy of life kept spilling out.

MY PATIENCE HAD bubbled over into frustration. The last patches of sunlight were flickering in the treetops. In another twenty minutes or so the few birds that still lingered in the sky would punch out for the day and the bats would start their shifts. Frannie had strategically positioned herself on a square of sidewalk close enough to the house to indicate her interest in coming inside but far enough away to prove that she hadn't yet reached a decision on the matter. I sat down on the outside steps and stared at the divided cap of black fur on top of her white head that reminded me of *Our Gang* star Alfalfa's slicked-down hairdo. How could I allow a cat with such a silly face to get the best of me? "If you don't come inside, I'm going to have to pick you up," I warned. She gave me an extended blink of satisfaction. Obviously, she didn't take my threat seriously.

The relaxed arc of her body on the cement was a far cry from the pulsing dynamo of nervous energy that had crouched beneath our bird feeder a few years earlier. Her back had twitched and flinched as she prepared to rocket away at the first shadow of movement from the people whose help she sought. Now when I took two paces in her direction, she yawned, rose to her feet, and in slow motion glided out of reach into the thick of Linda's flower bed. As soon as I returned to my spectator's seat on the porch, she ambled back to her spot on the sidewalk and showed her respect for my authority by turning her back and licking her tail. In a last-ditch attempt at doing things the easy way, I sprang to the top step, opened the door, and reasoned with her. "Come on Frannie. It's getting dark. Let's go."

Completely ignored, I slumped back down the steps. Although she was driving me crazy at the moment, I knew that I didn't have a whole lot to complain about. Yes, Frannie could be difficult to live with. Inside the house she required megadoses of reassurance. Outside the house she required a wheelbarrow load of being left alone. She bore no resemblance whatsoever to the snuggly-wuggly kind of kitty that I used to think I loved the best. In fact, she insisted on having more empty space around her than any cat I had ever known. But on those rare occasions when she waltzed up to me wanting to be petted, I felt like I had been given a gift.

Back in the latter half of the Pleistocene Epoch when we only had a single solitary cat, adding a second not unexpectedly doubled the burden. Taking on a third cat, though, only increased the labor and shed tears by 33 percent. Moving from three cats to four, five, and six should have involved incremental changes so that we would hardly even notice the additional aggravation. These weren't theoretical cats, however. These were Frannie, Maynard, and Tina. On a good day, Linda might complain, "You can't go anywhere in this house without stepping on a cat." On a bad day I could only console myself by contemplating my sister's lot in life. "At least we don't have *twelve* like Joan and Jack," I would say.

Faults aside—litter box mishaps, scuffles, dining room incursions, disturbed sleep, vet bills, food bills, damaged property, and our battered psyches—our cats were a companionable crew. Not a single day passed in which they failed to make us laugh. Even if a Buster Keaton video would have had the same effect, hugging a DVD fell a wee bit short of cuddling Moobie or Maynard.

RETREATING INTO THE house, I killed fifteen minutes leafing through the latest copy of the *New Yorker* and taking a shower. I scrubbed my hands at the sink to wash off any last residual traces of catnip and then I put on clean, catnip scent–free clothes. The kitty drug occasionally accentuated the uncooperative side of Frannie's mercurial personality, and I didn't want to take any chances.

I couldn't find her when I sat back down on the steps, but she emerged from beneath the hosta leaves to rub against my leg. Leaning backward on the step, I popped open the door behind me and held it open awhile.

"Let's go, sweetie," I told her.

Even on her most stubborn days, this nonchalant method of creating a point of entry usually coaxed her inside, but today she adamantly refused to abandon the amusement park of my shins. She didn't even scoot off when I lowered my hand to pet her. She buried her face in my fingers. Then she gave my leg the old-fashioned full-body-massage treatment by pressing against me as she sidled back and forth. I held off picking her up, hoping that she would finally hop up the steps on her own and ease onto the porch, but cooperation didn't appear to be on the evening's agenda. I hated to break her trust with a fast grab—so I decided upon a slow grab instead.

I warned her of what was to come by petting her with both hands, one on each side, and then I slowly increased the pressure. "Sorry," I told her as I tightened my grip and lifted her off her feet. To my astonishment, she didn't struggle when I held her to my chest. She leaned against me, laying her head on my shoulder and staying completely still as I stroked her neck. I expected her to freeze into stony panic as soon as I stood up, but I was able to hold her with one arm as I opened the door. She didn't bolt when I set her down on the porch floor or act aggrieved. She trotted over to her dish as if we hadn't done anything out of the ordinary and glanced up at me with a summons to pet her while she ate.

I couldn't remember the last time that she had surprised me this much. She hadn't simply tolerated being picked up. She had enjoyed it. In fact, I suspected that the entire point of the last forty minutes had been to manipulate me into carrying her into the house for reasons known only to her deep and peculiar self. Possibly she had seen me hauling the other cats around, and though they complained about the conveyance, what had registered with Frannie was that they were getting treatment that she wasn't. She wanted that same measure of closeness. At least she wanted to try it once. Like

Moobie wearing her collar after her surgery, she had taken what at first blush looked like a restriction and transformed it into a privilege.

SLEEPLESS IN THE middle of the night, on my way back from a glass of water I paused to pet a moonlight-framed Moobie on the head. I scratched her neck and left her purring so loudly I wondered that she didn't wake the other cats. In bed again, as I wiggled under the sheet I heard a thump above my head. A few moments later Lucy's raspy hiss from the front hall was answered by a low growl. Agnes must have jumped off my chair upstairs and trotted down the steps to see what I'd been up to. Straining to hear the details of their unusually hushed disagreement, I heard a distant muffled drumming as Maynard pummeled the door of Linda's study begging to come out. Tina was almost certainly on the rug directly behind him.

I thought of Frannie asleep on the porch, dead quiet but drowning out the sound of the other cats. I heard her dreaming that she was racing through the woods—alone in the world, but not for long. The ice crunched beneath her feet. Snow hissed in the air and flecked her fur. She ran in that unhurried but determined feline fashion with erect body, stiffly trailing tail, and legs flickering like the frames of a silent movie. The wind flattened the fur on her face. A cat on a mission, she moved to the rhythm of her breathing, ignoring the honk of a diesel horn and my rubbernecking wife's blue car grinding to a halt on the shoulder of the road. Squirrels, crows, coyotes, ferrets, minks, lemurs, hognosed snakes, and flying fox bats dispersed as her claws tore up the ground. She scattered her past into atoms as she ran. With the strength of a thousand beating hearts she was charging toward us and toward her happiness.

Acknowledgments and Culpability

· ·

SPECIAL THANKS TO Moobie for sitting on my lap and providing editing advice as I wrote this book—and to Linda for doing the real work in our house while I sat at my computer with Moobie on my lap. I owe Linda yet another debt for thinking up the title *Kitty Cornered* while soaking in the bathtub.

A solid gold kibble is earned by my good friend Bill Holm for managing to find his way into yet another book—thus assuring its success—by my sister Joan and her husband Jack for cat advice, and by my sister Bett for her love and support.

Big bowls of milk go to my agent, Jeff Kleinman of Folio Literary Management, and to my editor, Kathy Pories of Algonquin Books of Chapel Hill, for helping me to figure out how to best tell this story.

Most of all, I want to thank our beleaguered veterinarians for their excellent care of our critters over the years: Dick

Bennett, Laura Boge, Jason Chudy, Stephanie Dorner, Edward Farnum, Bruce Langlois, Raymond Leali, Kim Mast, Lawrence Nauta, and Bobbie Zech.

Special thanks to Wayne Schuurman at Audio Advisor, Peg and Roger Markle of Wild Life Rehab Center, Sjana Gordon of Lowell Farm and Wild Life Center, Brian J. O'Malley, Marcia Davis, Kathleen Schurman, Claire Bruno, Kelly Meister, Cayr Ariel Wulff, Mark Winter, Dave Hauger, Dennis Keller, and Phillip Hemstreet.

Hypnotic thanks to all of my readers who love *Kitty Cornered* so much that you're going to order copies of my other books right now.

Bob Tarte wrote the Technobeat world music column for *The Beat* magazine for twenty years. He has also written for the *New York Times,* the *Boston Globe,* the *Miami New Times,* the *Whole Earth Review,* and other publications. He hosts the podcast *What Were You Thinking?* for PetLifeRadio.com. Bob and his wife, Linda, live in Lowell, Michigan, and currently serve the whims of parrots, ducks, geese, parakeets, rabbits, doves, hens, and several cats. They also raise and release orphan songbirds for the Wildlife Rehab Center Ltd. For pictures of Bob's cats and other critters, visit BobTarte.com.